golden
scars

how the death of my husband
prepared me to battle breast cancer

emily
barry zarecki

Golden Scars:

How the Death of My Husband Prepared Me to Battle Breast Cancer

COPYRIGHT © 2024 BY EMILY B. ZARECKI

ISBN-13: 979-8-218-37800-4

For Steve, who I loved then, now, and always,
and our children, Steven, Emma, and Stella,
the light of my life.

For Mark, who lovingly embraced me - scars and all -
and whose love and support continue to help me heal and
move forward with purpose.

For Mom, who loved deeply, protected fiercely, and set the
perfect example that enabled me to be the mother, wife, sister,
and friend I am today. For Dad, my biggest supporter, my rock,
and my guiding light.

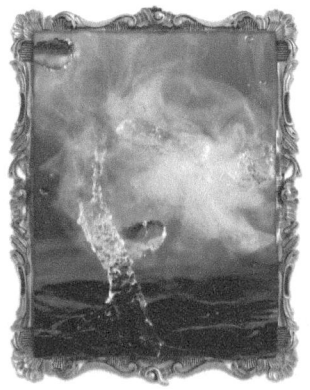

chapter one

When water first begins to boil, the surface appears still. But when you stand over the pot, you can see small bubbles rising to the surface. I feel something like that collision of bubbles in the pit of my stomach as I sit down at my desk and open my laptop.

A small trickle of sunlight falls through the window in my office. It's not enough to even see my keyboard, so I click on the quartet of lamps I have set up around my desk before opening my email.

I am distracted. Just waiting for the doctor's office to call. As I begin to wade through a long list of emails, all I see are reminders of my mammogram from last year—an appointment card for my follow-up tacked to the wall, a pink ribbon pin sitting at the edge of my desk. Cancer. It's just all cancer around me it seems. I can't focus on anything except the receptionist's words still reverberating in my memory.

I was buttoned up and ready to leave the doctor's office, nearing the checkout desk to schedule next year's mammogram, when the receptionist said something unexpected to me.

"The radiologist wasn't able to read your mammogram," she started with a kind smile—the kind people use to try and put you at ease. "Your breast tissue is dense, so I need to schedule you for a follow-up ultrasound."

My breast tissue is dense? I was caught off-guard. What does that even mean? And why wasn't it dense last year?

The receptionist read the look of panic on my face. "It's okay. The test is really easy, and the radiologist will read the test right away, so you'll know your results before you leave."

I knew she was trying to help me, but fears of breast cancer immediately began dancing around my head, and they didn't stop until the appointment.

When it came time for the ultrasound, my mother offered to go with me. She was in remission then, so she knew exactly what I would need, which was support, reassurance, and a "girlfriend day" for lunch to wind down afterward.

I walked into that dimly lit room with the narrow bed and the ultrasound machine. The tech instructed me to take my clothes off from the waist up and put on the hospital gown, so the opening was in the front. She asked me to lie down, and in a gentle voice, she asked me to raise my left arm above my head. Then she said, "I'm going to apply warm gel on the wand and move it around your breast to take the pictures." I took a deep breath and tried to relax. The test only took a few minutes.

As she was cleaning the machine, she handed me a towel and said, "Go ahead and get dressed. The radiologist will read the test, and we'll tell you the results in a few minutes."

I got dressed, sat down on the edge of the bed, and waited. I looked around the room, which was barely lit by a small light on the table across from me. It was so quiet. The minutes passed so incredibly slowly. I tried to stay calm, but my thoughts kept going dark. Breast cancer. Breast cancer. What if it's breast cancer?

Just then, the door opened, and the tech stepped back into the room. I noticed there wasn't anyone else behind her. Maybe that was a good sign. A doctor would certainly be the one to deliver bad news, right?

"Everything looked fine. Plan to have another mammogram next year."

With that, my shoulders relaxed.

"Thank you so much." I got up from the edge of the bed and walked back to the waiting room to share the good news with Mom. What a relief!

A year passes, and I find myself in that same white waiting room again, preparing myself to walk back into that dimly lit exam room and face the ultrasound machine. I recall that great feeling when I heard the words, "Everything looked fine." I tell myself everything will be the same this time around.

A woman in scrubs calls my name from the waiting room doorway. She guides me back to the ultrasound room. Immediately, I notice the room is a bit brighter than the room I was in the year before. Or maybe I'm just feeling a bit brighter this time.

I lay down, same as last time. She adds the warm gel to the ultrasound wand, explains how the test is done, same as last time. I lift my right arm over my head, and she places the wand on my right breast. She moves the wand to different spots on my breast and takes pictures. I think to myself, *Just like last time.*

Once she's captured the images she needs, she gives me a towel to wipe off the gel from my chest and asks if I'd like her to bring my husband back to wait with me. I say, "Yes, please," without hesitation.

Mark and I wait in silence while the radiologist reads the images. I try to slow my breathing. Sensing my nervousness, Mark reaches over and grabs my hand.

The door opens and the ultrasound tech begins to walk into the room.

Behind her, I see a woman in a lab coat also walking into the room. I see her name embroidered on the left side of her coat. It's a doctor. The radiologist. My breath catches.

"Hi, Emily," she says, and I introduce my husband to her. She shakes our hands, then walks to the monitor that displays an enlarged image of my breast tissue. My eyes zero in on a black circular spot on the image. She points to the spot and says, "There's a suspicious spot here. It looks like a small fibroadenoma—a benign mass. I'm almost positive that's what it is."

I breathe I sigh of relief. *Benign is good.*

But to be sure the small mass is a fibroadenoma, she adds, I need to have a biopsy.

I hear the clicks of the mouse and the tapping of keys as the receptionist finds time in the schedule for the biopsy.

We leave. It's quiet in my head, like static. As we walk down the stark hallway bathed in beige, I feel numb.

"...a benign mass. I'm almost positive that's what it is."

But what if it's not?

Mark walks ahead to bring the car to the entrance of the medical building. I look out the floor-to-ceiling windows as I wait. It's an incredibly dreary fall day—the sky is grey and a cold breeze rushes through the sliding doors of the medical building, chilling me to the bone.

As the car pulls up, I look in and see Mark give me a reassuring smile. I smile back and get into the car.

Mark grabs my hand and says, "It's going to be alright."

I push my tears away. "I hope so."

As soon as we get home, I walk straight to our bedroom and into the bathroom. I shut the door and look at myself in the mirror. I'm overwhelmed at the thought that there's this fibroadenoma inside me. I lift up my shirt and raise the right side of my bra off my breast. I bring my right hand up to the base of my breast. I slide my fingertips to the right. I gasp. *There's a lump.*

Even though I saw the black spot on the ultrasound monitor just thirty minutes ago, I thought it would feel different, like chunky Jell-O. This is hard and doesn't move. "Shit. Shit. Shit."

I'm panicking.

Mark is in the kitchen. I run up to him. "I felt it. There's something there."

Mark keeps a calm veneer. He speaks slowly, softly. His face is loose, his eyes kind. "The doctor said she's almost positive it's benign," he reminds me. His hands are on my shoulders.

I try my best to put the idea of a needle going into my right breast and into this lump out of my mind. The biopsy is in three days. It's supposed to be a beautiful fall weekend.

When we arrive at the women's center, I'm escorted to the same ultrasound room I'd just left a few days ago. The radiologist walks into the room to introduce herself and explain the procedure.

"Try to relax," she says. "I'll numb the area first. It's going to feel like little bee stings. Most women say it's the worst part of the whole procedure."

Little bee stings was exactly right. There is no better description for the sharp prickles of heat that ran through my breast.

The doctor wheels a small cart with supplies to the right side of the bed. "Are you ready?"

I look at her. I nod *yes*.

The needle enters the lower side of my right breast. I don't feel a thing, maybe a little pressure. After a few minutes, the biopsy is finished. The radiologist has the sample of what I pray is the benign fibroadenoma.

After I get dressed, there's a knock on the door. The tech peeks her head around and says, "We should have the results back in a couple of days. You'll get a call from your doctor's office."

So now, I wait.

I have a hard time putting the idea of the lump in my breast out of my mind. Instead of dwelling on the unknown, I try my best to immerse myself in my work and in the long to-do list on my plate—putting the final touches on a proposal for a new client, writing a blog post for our website, preparing for a team meeting to finalize a marketing strategy for a client, researching content for a talk I'll be giving at a conference in a couple of months. I turn away from that pink ribbon pin just sitting on my desk, tell myself to take a deep breath, and turn back to my work.

It isn't long before I'm suddenly jerked away from my focus on the proposal. Ding. I pick up my phone and see a notification from the hospital's patient portal. "There's a new test result."

Without a moment's hesitation, I click on the icon to open the patient portal app. The result from the biopsy is there. I feel my heart start to race. I click on the link and begin scanning, frantically scrolling through the report to find something that tells me this lump is benign. I can't make out much of the report. *Estrogen receptor negative, progesterone receptor negative.*

"Okay. Negative, negative. This is good."

"Right breast, 7 o'clock... rubbery tissue fragments."

I keep scrolling through the report. I don't understand all of the medical terms. It's like I'm trying to read something in a foreign language. Still, I keep scrolling toward the bottom and see the word "negative." Okay, I think, she was right. It is probably benign.

I go back to the proposal. A sense of relief washes over me. I feel my shoulders relax as I turn back to my computer.

The phone rings. It's my doctor's office calling now. Fear and anxiety take the place of relief.

"Hello?" I pause, waiting to hear Tracy's voice.

"Hi, Emily…" The voice continues speaking but I don't hear what she's saying. My mind goes blank. All I can think is that this isn't Tracy's voice. Tracy is always the one who calls me with negative test results. This is Grace, my nurse practitioner.

She begins talking, but I don't hear what she's saying.

Why is Grace calling me? It's supposed to be Tracy.

After a few seconds, I interrupt Grace mid-sentence.

"Did you just say I have cancer?"

chapter two

The sliding doors to the hospital ER open and I step into the busy lobby. *A number of visitors crisscross past me. Some are walking to the row of chairs in the waiting area while others are hurrying down a hallway, and others are stepping out the door to the parking lot. I approach the information desk and give the receptionist Mom's name.*

"She's in the last treatment room on the right," she says and pushes a button on the desk. A wide metal door opens, guiding me toward a hallway full of rooms. The nurse's station is buzzing with activity. Machines beep. Wheels on small carts carrying blood pressure machines scurry across the tile floor. Staff in scrubs move quickly in and out of treatment rooms. The hallway is abuzz.

I approach the last room on the right and push the curtain to the side. There's a look of angst on Mom's face. The doctor ordered a series of tests—ultrasounds and a CT scan of her abdomen—to try and find answers for the symptoms she's been dealing with for weeks. Her belly is swollen and in pain, she can't keep much down, and I've never seen her so tired. We need answers.

Amid all the frantic activity and loud voices in the next room over, "Code Blue," echoes overhead. Staff rush into another treatment room, while, at the same time, the ER doctor opens the curtain to my mother's bed and abruptly delivers the news.

Late-stage ovarian cancer.

"No," Mom cries out. She pulls her legs up to her chest into a fetal position and buries her face in her hands. I look at Mom—I look at her differently, deeply—and then over to Dad as the shocking news sets in. Mom looks back up at each of us in disbelief. She looks at us with fear.

Now, I am the one with cancer. At this point, Mark and I are the keepers of this unwanted secret. Mark wants to hold off telling the kids. I disagree. My gut tells me we need to share the news sooner rather than later, but there's also a part of me that wishes I could keep this dark enigma from the kids. As their mom, I've always wanted to protect them from bad things that happen. I know I can't protect them forever. Right now, nothing has changed. Their world is still the same as it was yesterday.

I walk in the kitchen to all three of my children, Steven, Emma, and Stella, quietly staring into screens and notebooks and books, doing their homework online. I look at each of them, think about the little lump growing in my chest, and my heart aches.

"We're headed out. Be back in a while," I say, and Emma perks up. Her brow furrows with suspicion.

"You're going to the doctor again? Why is Mark going with you?" she asks. Steven and Stella are looking at me now, too.

I make up an excuse about needing a follow-up test after my mammogram, like last year, and said that Mark wants to come along. That little white lie seems to satisfy her for the moment. It buys me more time, but I need to tell them soon.

The kids aren't so young that I need to share the news in words they'll understand. Steven is nineteen. He's laid back, thoughtful, caring, and so darn funny. We've always been incredibly close. Part of me feels that, given the fact he's in college studying nursing, I can tell him a bit more detail. He geeks out about all things medical, except we won't just be talking about breast cancer in general. I'll be telling him that I have breast cancer.

The twins, on the other hand, are fifteen. Their only experience with a loved one having cancer is my mom, their grandma. Although my type of cancer and stage is so different, I know they'll try to compare the two.

Emma is a lot like Steven when it comes to their personalities. She's sweet and has this spark that can light up a room. Her laugh is contagious. She's more athletic than her sister. For a few years, she took gymnastics lessons. As I watched her tumble across the floor or swing on the uneven bars during practices, I was transported back in time, remembering the years I took gymnastics lessons and competed on a team while I was in middle school. Her time with gymnastics was short-lived. She opted to try karate.

I've always called Stella my "old soul." She is kind, sensitive, and incredibly introspective. While her sister is athletically inclined, Stella excels in music and art. Drawing on sketch pads evolved into digital art on her iPad. She also spent a few years learning to play the violin. Much like my mom, she worries a lot. When she was about six years old, Stella overheard a story on the news about a few people in another part of the country contracting Ebola. These cases were nowhere near where we lived, but she was terrified of getting Ebola. That early experience may have been the start of her need to feed her intense curiosity on Google.

Later in the evening, the girls are upstairs in their bedrooms. Taking a deep breath, I climb the stairs. Lingering for a second at the door to Emma's bedroom, I walk in to find her sitting on her bed with her laptop in front of her. I call out to Stella to have her come to Emma's room. I notice the look of concern in their eyes.

"There's something I need to tell you," I pause for a second. "I know you guys have been aware that I've had a few doctor's appointments recently." They nod with looks of concern changing to fear.

I tell them about my mammogram and the follow-up tests.

"I have breast cancer."

Immediately, their eyes widen and begin to tear up. I try to reassure them, telling them we caught it early, but it's hard to comfort them in this moment, after hearing the words that their mom has cancer.

Figuring they may be thinking about their grandma's cancer, I say, "My cancer is not the same as what Grandma had. She had ovarian cancer, and it was caught very late. It was stage four. Mine is stage one."

Although I don't know anything about what treatment will look like yet, I try my best to comfort them. "I'm going to beat this," I say it as confidently as I can muster at this point.

They both nod without saying a word. I'm not sure what else to say. I'm still wrapping my head around it all myself.

"Promise me that you will come to me if you have any questions or if you want to talk about it more." Looking over to Stella, I say, "Don't go looking up articles on Google!" With a little smirk, she agrees.

I bring them both to me in a bear hug that I need just as much as they do. "I love you, girls. We'll get through this."

I walk downstairs and find Steven sitting on the couch, scrolling through his phone. I sit next to him and begin to share my news, much in the same way I had with the girls. While we're talking, I notice him grab his phone. His thumbs move feverishly across the keyboard on the phone's screen.

"You have the most common type of breast cancer," he says. Here, I figured Stella would be the first one to start Googling breast cancer!

He goes on to tell me that 70-80% of all breast cancers are the type I have—invasive ductal carcinoma—and that it responds well to treatment. I feel a sense of relief hearing that. "Of course, you'd get the most popular type of breast cancer!"

I roll my eyes and laugh.

Steven leans in for a hug, "You'll beat this."

Next, I need to tell Dad. I want to tell him in person. Just thinking about telling Dad brings an ache to the pit of my stomach.

As I walk up the steps to his front door, I take a deep breath. I peek through the window to the right of the door and see him sitting in the armchair in the living room, probably watching TV, as he does most evenings. He looks up and motions for me to come in.

The house is quiet except for the sound of Jeopardy coming from the TV. I walk slowly down the hall toward the living room. Each step feels like it echoes through the house. Before getting to the living room, I look left to see the master bedroom is dark. A once warm room where Mom spent many of the early days when she was first sick. Now, it's cold with the lingering memory of her.

Dad stands up and motions for me to sit down on the couch. I sit six feet away, as we're all accustomed to doing now because of COVID. Dad is high risk.

While we're making small talk, the pain in the pit of my stomach returns.

With a father's intuition, he senses there's a reason I'm visiting. "So, what's up?" he gestures for me to tell him what I'm clearly holding onto.

Here we go. "So, Dad. Do you remember last year, Mom came with me for an ultrasound after my mammogram couldn't be read?"

"Yes, I remember that," he says.

"Well, the same thing has happened again this year. I had the ultrasound, and the radiologist found a small mass. She said she was sure it was benign fibrous tissue but needed to do a biopsy to be sure. The results just came back," I take a deep breath. "I have breast cancer."

Dad pauses for a minute, looks over to me, and simply says, "Well, crap."

I recognize the distressed look on his face. There's been one other time when I saw the same look. *The hospice nurse came out from behind the curtain. Mom was asleep now. Our eyes were tired, and our faces were drawn with worry.*

We looked to the nurse for her assessment. "It's not going to get better," she said, looking down at her fumbling hands.

"How long?" Dad said.

"Maybe five days."

Five days.

"I really hate telling you, especially since it's not even been a full year since we lost Mom," I say, "but this is different. The doctor said we caught it very early."

In that year, Dad has been alone. Really alone. Because of the pandemic, activities he had been part of—weekly rotary club meetings, euchre at the senior center, Mahjong with his church group—have all stopped. Nothing is being held in person right now. He's in the house, day after day, alone.

The house he and Mom shared. "The silence is deafening," he tells me. I fully understand the expansiveness of that silence right now.

I go on to tell him that I'll know more after we meet with the oncologist in a couple of days. Verbalizing the word *oncologist* is weird.

We say goodbye from a distance. I can't even hug him now. I leave his house feeling ever-so-slightly relieved that he knows, and at the same time, burdened that he knows.

My thoughts shift from telling Dad I have cancer to attempting to comprehend the fact that I have cancer. The thoughts are so heavy. *Cancer.*

Cancer.

It's surreal. I don't physically feel any different. Aside from knowing there's this blueberry-sized lump at the base of my right breast, I feel fine. I don't feel any differently now than I did the morning I got the call from Grace and heard those three life-changing words: *invasive ductal carcinoma.*

I'm really not sure what to think or how to feel. It's this sense of numbness, of not having a clue about what's next. Images of what I think cancer patients look like overtake my thoughts—gaunt, bald, sickly-looking, weak.

I try to keep calm, on the outside at least. It's like quiet chaos. I'm doing my best to keep it together while my thoughts run wild. Pangs of anxiety are bubbling beneath the surface, about to boil.

I have cancer.

chapter three

I've had a surreal feeling like this once before. Nineteen years ago, to be exact. During my marriage to my first husband, Steve.

It's 5:30pm on a cold, dreary day in January. There are just a few of us left in the building. I sit at my desk. My office, at the end of the hallway, by the elevator, is lit by the soft light of a desk lamp. My back is to the window that overlooks the parking lot. I sit there, feeling numb. There's something nagging at me about the past weekend. Steve was unusually distressed about the strangest thing.

"It's no big deal," I told him. "We can call a plumber to help." But Steve was hell bent on figuring it out on his own. He wouldn't let it go. Couldn't let it go.

As I push my chair back from my desk and pick up my coat, the phone rings. I don't recognize the number. At first, I take a step away—spam call, wrong number, whatever—but then, something nudges me. I feel like I should answer the phone.

"Hello, this is Emily."

"Hi, Emily. My name is Karen Paul. I am a counselor at Dr. Able's office, a psychiatric practice in Toledo. Your husband is here with me."

My mind spins. What? I'm trying to grasp what she's saying, but I don't understand. Why is Steve there? He has seen a psychiatrist in Columbus to manage his depression for years, but he didn't mention he had an appointment with a new doctor.

She went on to say he was there for a crisis appointment.

Crisis.

During his appointment with this counselor, Steve talked about being in a deep depression that triggered dark feelings the past weekend. He admitted to the counselor what he planned to do.

Driving to the hospital for my first appointment with the oncologist felt very much like a crisis appointment. I think of Steve on the drive there. I feel numb, unsure about what's in store for me. My mind wavers between racing thoughts and going blank. I stare outside the car window. The other drivers are going about their lives, heading to work or running errands. I'm in a crisis. I'm scared.

I walk through the doors at the hospital and approach the registration desk to sign in for my appointment. After the receptionist confirms my information, she motions to her right. I look over and see big silver block letters that hang on the teal wall behind the desk: CANCER CENTER.

I've spent time in cancer centers before, but this is different. The last time I was at a cancer center for this same hospital system, I was managing a photoshoot that would be part of a marketing campaign to promote the hospital's oncology services. As a communications manager, I was used to being behind the scenes in different departments throughout the hospital, including chemo rooms and with big diagnostic machines.

This time, I'm on the other side. I'm not walking into this cancer center as a member of the marketing department. I'm not here to talk with the manager about patient stories we can highlight in our newsletter or in a video for an employee meeting. When I cross the threshold into the cancer center this time, I am the patient.

I am here to meet the oncologist as a patient with cancer.

I take a seat in the waiting room, facing the words CANCER CENTER. Along with the oncologist, I'll be meeting a surgeon, radiation oncologist, and physical therapist for a Breast Cancer Clinic. The idea is to meet with all of the specialists you may encounter during the treatment at once instead of scheduling separate appointments with each specialist. It's a great idea, in theory. The Breast Cancer Clinic is like "speed dating" with potential members of your healthcare team. Each specialist comes into the room and talks about their area of expertise and what to expect as a patient.

So many emotions feel like they're in competition with one another today. Anxiety. Fear. Grief.

In a single year, to the day, I've come to the other side of things.

I'm staring out the same window again. Day after day, I stare out this window, and then I look over at Mom. Still unresponsive. Day after day. But one thing is different today. The blaring noise of a leaf blower outside. I watch a man shove away dead leaves from the edge of the building, and I feel annoyed. It grows and grows inside of me as that leaf blower eats away at the serenity that is supposed to be the hospice center. I know Mom's not sleeping, she can't be woken up, but it's not the point. She still needs her peace! I'm yelling in my head when the doctor comes in.

The doctor listens to Mom's chest, comments that her breathing is still strong and steady, and reminds me that although she isn't awake, she can still hear us. I look at the leaf blower man. See? I think at him.

I lean down and give Mom a kiss on the cheek, whisper that I'm going to get lunch, reassure her that I'll be back soon. I need a reprieve from the sound of the leaf blower. From the constant and intrusive noise of it.

Lunch is a blur. I can't hear whatever Mark is saying. The day feels stretched thin, like I'm floating through it all. But there is a little tug inside me—something different and sharp—and I feel like I need to get back to Mom. I only want to be with my mom. And when I pull into the parking lot, I feel more at ease. The closer I am to her, the better.

I see my uncle walking down the hallway, coming toward me. I smile and hold out my arms to hug him. He wraps me up in his chest, but he isn't smiling. He's shaking.

"She's gone," he whispers.

On the one-year anniversary of my mother's death, I sit in an exam room, talking to an oncologist about a cancerous mass growing inside of me. How incredibly bizarre.

The exam room feels cold, sterile. With its high ceiling, pale walls, and hard plastic chairs, the setting doesn't evoke the warmth of comfort and reassurance I need. It does, however, align with the apprehension I feel about all of this.

The oncologist, Dr. Al, describes the different types of breast cancer. I just always thought breast cancer was breast cancer. He also talks about the standard courses of treatment for each kind—some requiring radiation, surgery, or chemo.

Chemo.

Two nurses cloaked in yellow gowns, hats, masks, and gloves double check the IV bags of medicine and compare them to the chemo meds on the order from Mom's doctor. Mom sits quietly, calmly. I'm struck by this—by how at ease she is while the nurses connect the tubing from the bags to the catheter in her arm. We sit casually, talking, like there aren't any toxins floating down that tube and into her body.

Dr. Al says my cancer is HER2+. It's an aggressive, fast-growing cancer. He describes how the cancer cells were fed by this HER2 protein. I'm trying my hardest to follow what he's saying, but I'm stuck on the word "aggressive." My mind drifts. I paint a picture in my head of these wild cancer cells opening their mouths and gobbling up proteins, like some sort of cancer Pac-Man. They're moving at a frenetic pace, finding as much protein as they can, all the while growing bigger and bigger.

I look at Dr. Al, at his mouth moving, but all I can hear are the questions forming in my mind: *If this cancer is aggressive, how fast is it growing? Will it grow into other areas of my body before I start treatment?*

My course includes three phases lasting one year.

One year.

He says the first phase will last four months. Hearing the word chemotherapy, I feel my heart sink.

Mom isn't sick. It's a few days out from chemo, and she's tired. She won't eat much. Can't, she says, but she isn't sick. I stick around. Expect her to start throwing up or writhing in pain, like you see in the movies. But none of that comes.

By the end of the second treatment, she's frail, but she isn't sick. Mom's hair is starting to fall out. She is graceful about this. I know it isn't easy for her, but she makes it seem like it is. Maybe there is pain. Maybe I just don't know about it. Mom is really strong through it all.

After chemo is done, I'll have a break. No treatment for at least four weeks before surgery to remove the mass. After surgery, there will be eleven rounds of immunotherapy and anti-cancer medication infusions. This process will span thirty-three weeks.

Listening to the explanation of this yearlong treatment plan is overwhelming. I feel the weight of it all as I try to shift around in my chair. Just picking up my right leg to cross it over my left feels like my leg is weighted with sandbags.

I don't want to go through chemo.

But if I want to get rid of this lump growing in my chest and keep it from spreading anywhere else, I have to.

I'll have two options for surgery. One is a lumpectomy, where the mass and a portion of tissue around the mass are removed. After the lumpectomy, radiation is required. The other option is a mastectomy, either single or both sides.

Sensing my uneasiness and shock, Dr. Al says that if we follow the treatment plan—chemo, followed by surgery, and then the infusions of the two medications—I'll have a 95% chance of being cured. He repeats that last statement for emphasis. "I'm not just saying the cancer will be treated. I'm saying there's a 95% chance that you will be *cured*."

I ask if it's possible to skip the chemo and have surgery first. The answer was a short one: "No." Dr. Al reminds me that the order of the treatment protocol of chemo, surgery, and immunotherapy is what yields the 95% cure rate.

So, that's what I *have to do to* beat this. I just don't want to go through chemo. I shudder at the thought of harsh, toxic drugs coursing through my body to kill the cancer cells. Unfortunately, they'll kill any fast-growing cells in their way—GI tract, hair, and nails.

I do believe in science and medicine. I have trust and faith in my doctor.

Medicine and therapy. Medicine and therapy. I've heard this before.

The psychiatrist diagnoses Steve with bipolar II depression and says that with a combination of medication and counseling, there is a great path forward that's possible. We put our trust and faith in the doctor and in the treatment. I have trust and faith in Steve.

But medication can be fickle, and there came a time when Steve felt like the medications might not be working as well as they once did. His psychiatrist tried other medicines. Over the course of six months, she tried four different antidepressants.

But Steve wasn't doing well. Depression had a strong grip on him, and it was the second time I felt so scared. He had been suicidal before. He hadn't done anything, but the dark thoughts were there.

Our dear friend and the pastor of our church, Father Dave, comes to see Steve at our house. He speaks to Steve with such care and tenderness. With a deep concern, he eloquently asks Steve a question that is difficult for any of us to broach. Gently, lovingly, Father Dave asks Steve if he plans to harm himself.

I look at Steve. He looks in a daze.

A second later, Steve suddenly snaps out of it, and with the whip of his head and conviction in his eyes, he says, "No, I would never do that. I'd never leave my family."

Despite his words, seeing Steve like this—like an empty shell; like he is drowning inside himself—is beyond frightening. I feel so helpless, but I let his words comfort me the best I can. I feel hope that we will get through this. I felt hope that his doctor will find a medicine that works. That's all I can do. Hope.

Medicines work differently and can have different effects on people, and I hope they'll be easy on me. I still wonder, *How will the chemo affect me? Will it work?*

If a 95% cure rate means that I have to go through chemo, surgery, and infusions, then that's what I'll do. I don't like the idea of it. I'm terrified of it, but I'll do it.

I've read articles and heard people speak about the connection between the mind and the body. Although I don't know what I'm in for, I know having a positive attitude will make a big difference.

I decide I need a mantra—something positive I can focus on and repeat during this next year. I rack my brain for phrases, but nothing resonates with me. *It will come to me,* I assure myself. I stop trying to force it.

There's a big envelope in the mail. It's from my brother and sister-in-law. There's a beautiful silver bangle bracelet inside with an inscription on the inside. It reads, "Fate whispered to the warrior, 'You can't withstand the storm.' The warrior whispered back, 'I am the storm.'"

That's it. That is my mantra.

I am the storm.

I. Am. The. Storm.

chapter four

The treatment plan has been set. I'm in this for one year. Chemo, surgery, more infusions. By the end of next year, I pray I'll be part of that 95% cure rate. Those are some very good odds! (Positive mindset, check.)

First up are six rounds of chemo. During each round, four drugs are administered by IV once every three weeks. I do the math in my head. Eighteen weeks. That's more than four months.

Taxotere. Carboplatin. Herceptin. Perjeta.

Taxotere and Carboplatin are the harsh chemo drugs I'll be getting over the course of eighteen weeks. The other two drugs are the immunotherapy and anti-cancer regimen. I'll be getting seventeen rounds of those. Dr. Al says Herceptin and Perjeta don't have cruel side effects, like the other two.

"This first part of treatment will be the hardest, but you'll get through it," Dr. Al says.

Because my cancer is aggressive, he wants to begin chemo as quickly as possible. Hearing that is scary. Those questions come racing in again: *How fast is the cancer growing? How much will it grow before chemo starts in a few weeks? Will it spread somewhere else?*

Ahead of the surges of these cruel but necessary medicines, I need to have an MRI and a port placed in my chest. Dr. Al describes how the port works and exactly where it will be.

Mom crosses her sweater over her chest, looks aways from me. "It's okay," I tell her. "It doesn't bother me." I pull her sweater aside for the nurse. The port protrudes from beneath her stretched and pale skin. I look it over before the nurse inserts a needle into the center.

"It looks ugly," Mom says.

"No, it doesn't," I lie to her.

I'm looking at a port now, before it's been put beneath my skin. Dr. Al turns it in his hands as I examine its parts. The port looks like a round disk with a long tail. It will be the bridge between the drugs in the IV bags and my veins.

A volunteer walks with me to the Interventional Radiology department. I change into the all-too-familiar hospital gown. My hands shake a little as I tie the gown closed in front of me. There's a knock on the door. "They're ready for you."

The radiology tech opens the door for me and we walk into the room. I'm struck by the freezing temperature of the room. The look of the room is cold, too. A clinical OR with a large x-ray machine. The tech guides me to the long x-ray table donned with blankets. She helps me get onto the table and as comfortable as possible. Despite her efforts, nothing can change that I'm lying on a metal slab. She puts a foam wedge under my knees and steps away. I stare at the ceiling, quietly praying that the procedure goes well, while staff in scrubs scurry around the room, finishing pre-procedure tasks.

"This will be over soon," I whisper to myself.

I try deep breathing.

Breathe in 1, 2, 3, 4... and out 1, 2, 3, 4, 5, 6.

The tech returns to my side and lays a warm blanket on top of me. It's like a comforting hug, and I need it right then.

The radiologist approaches the table and explains how the procedure will go, starting with a few injections of local anesthetic to the left side of my chest. The first injections go in about an inch below my collarbone. A few more injections go in a few inches above that, at the base of my neck.

The needle pricks aren't bad, but as the doctor slowly pushes the anesthetic through the needle, the bees are back, stinging me all at once.

I take a few more deep breaths and repeat to myself, "This will be over soon."

Throughout the forty-five-minute procedure, I didn't feel any pain. Just sensations of tugging and pressure, until all of a sudden, I started to feel hot and dizzy.

I feel like I'm going to pass out.

I picture Steve, imagining him standing in the room with me.

His latest medication had proven to be a difficult adjustment. I closed the bathroom mirror and looked myself over, ready for work, when I noticed Steve sitting on the bed with his back to me. He was still and quiet.

I sat next to him and put my hand on his arm. Feeling his soft skin, I looked at him and asked what was wrong.

"I'm not feeling that well. I think I'm going to take the day off. I haven't been sleeping well. I just want to get some rest." He said it gently, without looking at me, and with a sadness in the middle of him.

"I get that," I said softly. "With the kids at your mom's house, you'll have plenty of quiet time to get some sleep." Steve nodded in agreement and headed downstairs.

I found him lying on the couch with a light blanket draped over him as I headed out the door.

This will be good, *I thought.* He needs this. *I leaned down and kissed him goodbye. "Maybe you'll feel up to fishing later," I said with some hope. Being on the lake always did wonders for him.*

Steve grasped my hand. "Maybe," he said with a shy smile.

I walked out the door feeling comforted by the fact that Steve would be safe at home.

"Are you doing okay? Emily?" One of the techs leans over and encourages me to take some more deep breaths. Her calm voice is reassuring.

I focus on my breathing.

"The port is in," the radiologist says. "You feel alright?"

I nod my head yes. With a huge sigh of relief, I feel like I've made it through the first level of some horrible game. I relish this small victory.

Having the port placed is one step closer to the next level—the start of chemo.

I remind myself, "I am the storm," but I'm not convinced of that yet.

I can tell I have work to do before I can embody that mantra and head into this battle with the positivity I know I need to get through it.

chapter five

It's a dreary day. Gray clouds fill the sky. A cold breeze moves the naked branches on the trees. A chill in the air signals winter is coming.

Between putting on makeup and getting dressed, I step out of the bathroom to double check the tote bag laying on my bed that I've packed for the hospital. I check the side pocket and find a small tube of sunscreen—a sure sign it's been a while since I've used this bag. Instead of packing a beach towel and flip flops, I'm filling it with magazines, my iPad, earbuds, a charging cord, a blanket, new slippers embroidered with a beautiful cardinal, mint gum, and lemon drops.

I pick up the bag, turn off the light to the bathroom, and walk out to the kitchen. Mark and the kids are there. I see the look of concern in their eyes.

"You've got this, Mom," Stella says.

Steven, Emma, and Stella walk toward me and give me a big hug. I want to linger in this warm, comforting embrace, but it's time to go. Mark gently nudges me. With a slight nod, I hug the kids again. That dull ache I've been feeling in the pit of my stomach for the past couple of weeks gets stronger.

I don't want to do this.

Anticipating what my first chemo treatment will be like is overwhelming.

Will I feel sick right away? Did Mom feel sick all along?

I try to stop the flood of questions invading my mind. It's not easy. I don't know what I'm in for, but what I do know is that I've got to go into it with a positive attitude. That's got to have an impact on how my body handles treatment, right?

Come on, Emily, you've got this, I say to myself.

You are the storm, remember! I commit to talking myself up for this entire drive to the hospital.

Yes! I am the storm! I can feel it now.

I am the storm.

Then Mark turns on his signal to take the exit off the highway. I look to the left and see the hospital. Pangs of anxiety rise again.

As we pull up to the entrance of the hospital, I put on my mask.

"I'll park the car and be right in," Mark says with an assuring touch on my shoulder.

Every step from the car to the registration desk feels ominous. There

34

are people moving around me, screens and machines and people calling things out over a PA system, but I can't decipher any of it. The static sets in again. I say my name to the woman behind the desk. After confirming my information, she says, "You're here to see Dr. Al followed by treatment upstairs." Just like that. Like it's simple.

The reality of it all sets in. I feel like someone just put a huge, weighted yoke across my shoulders.

"Yes," I respond. Just like that. Like it's simple.

My first appointment begins in the small lab at the Cancer Center. The lab tech tells me a nurse will access my port and draw some blood through it. After cleaning the area where my port is, the nurse tells me to lean back in the chair and take a deep breath. I feel a forceful poke in my upper chest. The sensation is a lot stronger than a needle going in your arm. A small clear tube with the covered connecting point dangles from my port, ready to be joined to the IV bags filled with chemo drugs that await me upstairs.

The tech guides me back to the exam room. Mark is there, idly playing a game on this phone. He looks up and smiles as I walk into the room, and I sit next to him. After a few minutes, there's a knock at the door. Dr. Al steps in and greets us.

"Good morning. So, your first chemo today? How are you feeling about that?" he asks. He's trying to be jovial, positive—and so am I—but it's not working. Not really.

"I'm really nervous. I just don't know what to expect," I fidget as I say it. I can feel anxiety shifting around my body, making me scoot this way and that.

It feels like I'm taking a step into a room that's completely dark. I can't even see my hand in front of my face. I need to keep putting one foot in front of the other and have faith that the chemo will shrink this lump growing in my chest.

"You will get through it," he says. "You won't feel any different as the drugs are going in. The initial side effects usually take a few days to set in. You may be fatigued at first. It's hard to predict what will happen after that. Everyone reacts to the chemo differently."

I shake my head. "I get that." I start to calm down.

"So, what's your plan for your hair?"

What? Completely caught off guard by his question, I sit frozen for a few seconds. I know it's highly likely I will lose my hair. I'm coming to grips with that, but I'm also really dreading it.

I need to process it still. I've got some time, though.

Mom had a few chemo treatments before her hair started to fall out. I sit across from her hospital bed and watch as she flips through a magazine.

"Would you come over and brush through my hair? It's been so long since I've had a real shower. I've had to use those," she says, pointing to a shower cap. The label on the packaging reads, "cleansing shower cap." I don't even know what that means. An oxymoron, I think.

I pick up her brush and gently work it through her hair. As I get to the end of her short hair, I notice more hair than usual has collected between the bristles. I show Mom the brush.

"I figured I'd probably start losing my hair." She's so matter of fact. Nonchalant. It all seems so easy for her.

I tell Dr. Al that Mark and I have started talking about it. Since I'm continuing to work through treatment, I want to look for a wig that looks like the way I wear my hair—dark brown, straight, just above shoulder length. I also want to look at scarves and other head coverings to wear around the house. I can't imagine myself without hair. "I've got a little time, though. Isn't that right?" I ask.

"Fifteen days after the first treatment is typically when people start to see their hair fall out," Dr. Al says.

"WHAT? *Fifteen days?"*

A feeling of sheer panic consumes me. I feel robbed of more time... time to process all this. I know losing hair is a common side effect, but now that it's happening to me, fifteen days is so fast. I didn't expect it to be so soon after starting treatment. *I'm not ready.*

I know it's hair and it will grow back, but my hair feels so much a part of who I am, and knowing I'll lose it in just two weeks sends me spiraling. It's almost as if the shock of hearing I'll lose my hair in fifteen days is worse than learning about my diagnosis.

In an instant, I feel surrounded. I feel unlike anything I've ever felt before, like I'm treading water in the open sea. Sharks are circling me. Cancer surrounds me.

There is a part of me that wonders if it was my time.

On my mom's side, my grandmother and her sister both had cancer. Grandma's was breast cancer and her sister had ovarian cancer. Mom had ovarian cancer. My cousin, Ally, who is ten years younger than I am, had breast cancer. She is a survivor. On my dad's side of the family, my grandfather, my dad, and his three brothers all had different forms of cancer.

Cancer surrounds me.

I am drowning.

The shock of losing my hair also leaves me feeling incredibly vulnerable. Right now, no one knows I have cancer. After I lose my hair and start wearing a scarf to cover my bald head, I'll be branded a cancer patient.

I'll be cancer.

That's all anyone will see.

It feels like I'm being thrown into the deep end of the pool with no flotation device.

I've been dropped into the deep end once before. I've felt like I nearly drowned just one other time.

I worked until about 2:30pm that afternoon. My boss, who was well aware of the struggles Steve had been having, encouraged me to go home early to spend some uninterrupted time with Steve.

As I drive down the road to our house, I pray that Steve has been able to get some sleep and is feeling better. When I get closer to our house, I notice his black truck isn't in the driveway.

With some relief, I am glad to see the truck is gone. That means that he must have felt well enough to go fishing.

I pull into the driveway and press the button on the garage door opener. Nothing happens.

I try again. Nothing.

"Seriously?" I say out loud, irritated. "We just put new batteries in this thing."

I park the car and get my bag out of the backseat. I walk to the side door of our garage and grab the handle. Locked. In all the time we've lived in this house, we've never locked this door.

Confused, I peer through the glass on the top half of the door. I can see a taillight and the back of Steve's truck.

"No." A panic violently rises through my body.

No, this isn't what you're thinking.

Steve's truck has never been in the garage. He never keeps it in the garage. I don't know why the truck would be in the garage now... with the garage door closed and the side door locked.

"No. No. No."

I run around the garage to the front of the house and unlock the door. As I step into the house, I am overwhelmed by the smell of gas.

"Oh, God. No." I throw my bag down and look to my left, at the door that leads to the garage.

"No, that's not what's happening. There's another reason for this smell. That's not what's happening." I'm trying to convince myself; come up with other theories. My mind races.

I quickly scan the kitchen and living room. I run upstairs and into each room. First, the girls' room. Empty. Then, Stevie's room. Empty. Then, to our bedroom and bathroom. Empty.

I'm just running. From room to room, except to the one room I need to go in.

I think, We have a propane tank. Maybe something's wrong with it. That could be it. That's the smell.

I run downstairs to our family room and to Steve's office. He isn't there. Empty.

Back in the kitchen, I start pacing.

I have to look in the garage, *I tell myself.* I have to. *I keep pacing.* But I don't want to.

I turn to look at the door to the garage. I pray out loud, "Please, don't let this be what it seems like it is." My hand shakes as I grab the door handle. I turn it and open the door.

Steve is there, sitting in the front seat of his truck. His head is leaned back on the headrest. It looks like he's sleeping.

I gasp. "No!"

I slam the door closed.

I pace again.

What am I supposed to do?

Is he okay?

Oh, God! I'm so scared.

I run back to the kitchen, pick up the phone and dial my mom's number. As I listen to the ringing sound, I realize I am shaking.

Voicemail.

"Seriously?"

What do I do?

As the reality of what I think is happening sets in, I pick up the phone again and dial 911.

"911, what's your emergency?"

"Hello. I just got home from work, and I think... I think my husband killed himself."

I want to vomit.

Did I just say those words? "I think my husband killed himself."

"Where is he?" she asks.

"In the garage. He's in his truck."

"Is he breathing?"

"I don't know. I was too scared to go up to him when I first got home."

"It's okay, honey. Do you think you can go up to him now? I'll be right here on the phone with you."

"I'll try. I'm so scared. I don't know what's happening."

I walk toward the door to the garage again. I open the door and look at Steve.

I am struck by how peaceful he looks.

"Okay, I see him," I say.

"Can you go up to him?"

My legs feel like lead. I can't move.

"I want to, but I'm so scared."

"I'm right here on the phone with you. Can you see if there's a pulse?"

I try to move my legs, but I feel frozen in place.

"I'm scared. And it smells so bad in here," I tell her.

"You need to get out of the house now!"

I desperately want to go up to Steve. Why am I so scared?

"You should be hearing sirens soon. A sheriff will be there first. Other help is on the way, too."

I run out the front door.

"I hear the siren," I say.

"Okay, the sheriff will be there soon. Do you want me to wait on the phone with you?"

"No, that's okay. Thank you."

I walk to the side of my car and fall to my knees sobbing. How can this be happening?

The sheriff pulls in the driveway, parks his car, and quickly walks toward me. I stand up, wiping away the tears.

"You need to walk to the end of the driveway," he demands.

"But my husband is in the garage. I wanted to go up to him, but I was scared."

With a stern tone, he says, "Ma'am, you need to go to the end of your driveway."

With that, he runs up to the house. I am left alone. I don't know what is happening. I'm not allowed to go to Steve.

I am alone.

As I walk along the rough gravel of our driveway toward the road, I see two of my neighbors walking in my direction. Looking up at the sheriff's car, Nonni asks what's going on. Uttering the words, "I think Steve is dead," makes me feel sick to my stomach.

"No, no, no," Naomi says. "Oh my god, no," Jennifer says in disbelief. Nonni and Jennifer get to me and hug me at the same time. We hold each other in a group hug as tears fall down my face.

"I need to get a hold of my parents." I dial my mom's number again. She answers. In the way I say, "Mom," she knows something is wrong. I take a deep but shaky breath. Again, I verbalize this nightmare that's unfolding before me.

"No, oh Emily, no. We're on our way. We'll be there as fast as we can."

More first responders arrive at our house—police, firefighters, and EMTs. A firetruck, ambulance, and another emergency vehicle line the road. I see my dad's Jeep navigate the narrow path between the trucks and other vehicles. He parks the car in the grass at the edge of the driveway. I run up to my mom and dad. Mom reaches out to hug me. Her embrace feels so strong, so protective. But she can't protect me from what's happening. I relay what I came home to, how I searched the house for Steve, but found him in the garage.

I look past my mom and stare at the ambulance. A firefighter approaches the passenger side of the ambulance and talks with the EMTs. The EMTs aren't getting out of the ambulance. If Steve was still alive, they'd be rushing out of the ambulance and running up the driveway to assess him. Instead, the ambulance idles. I keep watching. Looking for any sign that can give me a glimmer of hope that Steve is alive. The firefighter steps away from the ambulance and hits the side of the truck two times with his hand. With those two taps, the ambulance drives away.

My heart sinks. There's no glimmer of hope to be had. Steve has to be dead.

I'm numb. I turn to face the house. I watch the people standing outside the garage. It's like watching an episode of a police drama. But this isn't a television show. It's not a story of fiction. It's really happening. A woman with long blonde hair and wearing plain clothes approaches me. She introduces herself. She's a detective.

She asks me all kinds of questions—from a step-by-step recollection beginning with what happened from the time I pulled into the driveway, the name of the doctor Steve was seeing and medications he was taking, to Steve's social security number. I stand there motionless, like a robot, answering her questions. While we're talking, I hear the sound of a motorcycle coming down our road. I don't think anything of it. That is until the motorcycle pulls into the driveway. The man on the motorcycle steers it up the driveway and parks the bike next to the sheriff's car.

"Who is that?" I ask.

The detective looks over her shoulder. "Oh, that's the coroner."

That's the coroner? A guy driving a motorcycle without a helmet... is the coroner? Of course it is!

The detective excuses herself to talk to the coroner. As she walks away, I am still, grasping to understand how my world has been completely shattered. I left for work concerned about how Steve had been feeling yet hopeful we'd get through it, like we had before. Ironically, I thought he'd be in the most comfortable and safe place—our home.

chapter six

Beginning chemo feels very much like I'm alone again. Although Mark is there. My doctor and the nurses at the infusion center are there and can help me get a sense of what to expect, but I'm on my own. While my family's love and support envelopes me, I'm stepping onto this path of treatment by myself. The drugs will be going into *my* system. They'll attack the cancer cells in *my* body. At the same time, they'll harm *my* healthy cells. The uncertainty of what's ahead for me is debilitating. Mark sits across from me in the small waiting room, yet I feel detached. I'm frozen with fear. It's like I'm sitting on an iceberg that's broken free from a glacier. I can see Mark, but I'm floating away. I'm about to face something dark and scary, something I've never experienced before. I will be the only one feeling the effects of the chemo.

When my name is called, I snap out of my dark thoughts. Mark and I walk through the door to the infusion center. A kind nurse greets us. I feel like I'm being led through a room that's completely dark. I can't see my hand in front of my face. I've tried to prep myself for this first chemo treatment, but I have nothing to compare it to, nothing to gauge how I'm going to feel. I know I have to trust this part of the process, but it's incredibly scary.

golden scars

I am the storm.

The nurse escorts us through the treatment area to my assigned spot. Each "room," like a mini exam room, has a recliner, a chair with an ottoman, a small TV, and a tray table. The treatment spaces are separated by three half-sized walls. The short walls give some sense of privacy, yet I can still look across the room and see someone else receiving their infusion. I can hear the sound of TVs in other treatment spaces.

We get settled in the room and I take a seat in the recliner. At our pre-chemo education meeting with one of the nurses, she told us to anticipate the first treatment lasting about five hours. I feel anxious. The idea of being here for five hours is daunting. That's like sitting through multiple full-length movies, or a football game that goes into overtime, or more than a half day of work, or five church services, or two full concerts, or a flight across the country.

The nurse returns and explains how the infusion will go. First, I'll receive the pre-meds—two medicines to prevent nausea and a steroid. The four drugs—Taxotere, Carboplatin, Herceptin, and Perjeta—will run separately this first time to make sure I don't have a reaction to any of them. It will take about forty-five minutes for each drug to be administered.

I try to keep calm, but it's all so overwhelming. I know, ultimately, chemo will be a tiny speck of paint on the full canvas of my life. But it will also drastically change everything about me.

I remind myself of my own strength; that I've gone through difficult things. Brutal, intense things. I think about Mom, and the grace she carried herself with. I think about Steve. The man I thought I was going to grow old with. I think about his courage—how he did everything he could to get well, how it must've felt like the disease was stronger than he was, how depression took him away from us so quickly. I think about the young woman I was then, left with three small children to raise alone. Stevie was eight and the girls were only four. And when I see their little faces in my mind, I also remind myself of who they've become. Steven now in college, the girls in high school. Happy. Brilliant. Driven. I smile.

"You can do this," I tell myself. "It's probably not going to be easy." I shake my head, "No, it won't be easy, but you will get through it." My attitude starts to shift, so I double down. "Remember, you are badass. You are the fucking storm!"

My inner pep talk was helping, until two nurses came into my cubby of a treatment room. They are dressed in long yellow gowns, masks, and gloves. It reinforces the danger of it all. The toxicity of the chemo. My nurse reads the name of the drug and the dose on the computer screen. They both look at the label on the IV bag to confirm I'm getting the right medicine and the right dosage. With a swipe of her badge on a digital reader near the keyboard, the second nurse agrees it's the right medicine for me and walks away.

"Okay, are you ready to get this started?" she asks with a gentle tone.

"No," I look up at her, "but let's do this."

As the chemo begins to course through my veins, I keep hearing Dr. Al say, "Fifteen days." Fifteen days until I lose my hair. I picture women, like Mom, who've gone through chemo. I think about cancer patients in movies—always thin and gaunt with pale skin.

Will I look like that? I wonder.

Scarves and head coverings that veil a bald head are kind of like a scarlet letter, and I don't want some wrap or hat brandishing me a cancer patient.

What if I don't lose my hair? I'm not trying to be vain. Hair is just part of who we are. Even though I disliked my hair growing up. I had thick brown, curly hair, but I desperately wanted straight hair. All of my friends had straight hair. With the help of chemicals, round brushes, and a flat iron, I wear my hair straight now. Part of me hopes I'll be in the small percentage of people who don't lose their hair from chemo. It's unlikely, though. Both of the harsh chemo drugs list hair loss as a top side effect.

If I've only got fifteen days, I better figure out what I'm going to do... and fast. So, I grab my iPad and start searching for wigs.

I want to find one that looks like the way I wear my hair. I want to look like myself, or as much like myself as possible. I'm not going to tell my clients yet, so I want it to look like nothing has happened. I search multiple sites trying to find one that's straight, dark brown, with an angled bob.

As I come across ones I like, I turn my iPad to show Mark. He nods in agreement. With a little grin, Mark suggests I look for one that's different from my usual hairstyle.

"Have some fun with this," he says. "Play around with some different looks. Maybe find one that's red!"

"Seriously?" I snap.

More than a little annoyed, I remind him I'm trying to look the same as I always do. When I wear the wig, I want to look in the mirror and recognize the reflection staring back at me. At least, recognize her as much as possible.

I'm sure he's trying to lighten my mood. He's good at that. I appreciate it, but I turn my head back to the tablet screen to resume my search.

I hear Dr. Al in my head again, "Fifteen days." The next thought hits me like a bomb.

My next treatment is three weeks from today. That's twenty-one days.

I am going to lose my hair before my next treatment.

An alarm on the IV pole snatches me away from my thoughts about the dread of losing my hair so soon. I look up and see the plastic of the IV bag has collapsed on itself. It's empty. The first drug is done. All of the medication is inside my body now. The nurse returns and switches out the IV bags. She hangs the second bag for chemo drug number two to begin.

Time at the infusion center is a funny thing. It's like there's an elasticity to it. With each drug running in forty-five-minute increments, time feels like it passes both quickly and at a snail's pace.

Nurses casually move about the infusion center, checking on patients and starting IVs. There are muted conversations between patients and their visitors. Sounds of Rachael Ray, game shows, and HGTV mingle in the air.

A stern voice rises above the quieter throngs of sound filling the treatment center. It's a man in the treatment cubby next to mine.

"Is Tom on yet? While we wait for any others to join, will you please turn on your cameras?"

Mark and I lock eyes. "Is that guy really leading a meeting here?" I whisper.

"We're going to resume our lesson from Monday," he says.

"He's teaching a class? From here?"

His cacophonous lecturing is ruining the chill vibe I need right now. I need a calm and relaxed exterior to combat the chaos and violence I feel internally. Toxins flow into my body, set to attack the cancer cells and any fast-growing cell in their path. It's pretty easy to tune out the sounds of other TVs or conversations, but this patient-teacher is speaking so loudly that it's nearly impossible to ignore.

As the last of the final drug flows through the line to my port, the nurse returns to disconnect the lines. There's a quick feeling of freedom... before I remember the drugs are now inside my body. I have a word with them.

Like a silent prayer, I tell the chemo drugs to do their thing.

"Go to my body where this small tumor is. Kill it. While you're attacking the cancer, please be kind to the rest of my body."

Before I'm given the green light to leave, the nurse prepares a patch with a medication to boost my immune system.

Once the nurse injects the medicine into the small reservoir on the patch and replaces the cover, I hear a beeping sound. She tells me that a tiny needle will poke the skin and insert a little catheter in my arm. Then, twenty-seven hours later, the medicine will self-administer.

"Why twenty-seven hours?" I ask. She laughs and says she doesn't know!

She applies the patch on my upper arm. After a few seconds, the beeping gets faster. And faster. I wait for the poke of the small needle. *Click. Poke.*

"Damn!" Without fail, I jump when it pokes me. I knew it was coming, but I still jump in my seat. It feels like the snap of a rubber band against my skin.

I hate this weird sadistic patch already.

The nurse tells me I'll likely feel the effects of the Neulasta, the immune system boosting drug, first. The most common symptom is bone pain.

"Bone pain? Well, that sounds awful."

"Claritin actually helps a lot," she says.

"Claritin, as in the allergy medicine?" I ask, making sure I heard her right.

She tells me it has helped ease the bone pain for other patients. I'll absolutely give it a try.

After five hours at the infusion center plus the time with Dr. Al, I am ready to go home. As soon as I walk from the garage into the kitchen, I see Steven, Emma, and Stella sitting in the family room. They each get up and walk toward me.

"Wait, guys. Give your mom a chance to get in the house," Mark says.

I understand Mark wanting to be protective, but I speak up. "No," I say. "It's okay. I'll never turn away hugs!" Holding the three kids in an embrace, I wish I can stop time to relish in just this moment.

I sit with the kids in the family room. They ask questions about the chemo and ask how I'm feeling. I really don't feel any different right now. Maybe a little tired, but that's all.

Side effects from the chemo are supposed to start about five days after treatment. It's a weird wait and see. It's like going into a haunted house. It's dark except for some lights to guide your path. You know people dressed in costumes will jump out at you, but you don't know when it will happen. You know there will be screaming and other loud sounds. So, you walk slowly and ambivalently into the house and through the dark rooms to find out what horror awaits you.

I wake up feeling good. I slept well. Like any other weekday, I get up and hop in the shower. The warm water feels good as it hits my back when I first get in. I step into the center of the shower and feel the water drench my hair. *Fifteen days.* I try to push that thought out of my mind as I shampoo my hair.

When I'm done with my shower, my thoughts turn to coffee. I see Mark sitting on the couch watching the morning news as I walk out of the bedroom.

"Good morning, sweetie. How do you feel?" A smile stretches across his face.

"I feel good. It's strange to think I had chemo yesterday. I don't feel any different today," I say with an anxious laugh. As I put the coffee pod in the Keurig machine, Mark reminds me to take it easy today. I promise him I will. I love how concerned and protective he is.

Back in the bedroom, I finish getting ready for work. Makeup. Dry my hair. Get dressed. Start the "commute" to work. Really, it's just a descent down the stairs to my desk in the basement.

I open my laptop. It's so surreal. *Chemo coursed through my body yesterday. I don't feel any different. Not at all.*

Throughout the day, co-workers send emails and instant messages asking how I'm doing. With each message, I do an internal check. *How am I feeling? Do I feel any different?* Nope. Such a strange dichotomy between chemotherapy yesterday and my normal workday today. Yesterday, I sat in a recliner with a line connecting an IV bag with toxic chemicals to my port that's connected to my arterial vein. Today, I'm working like it's any other workday—answering emails, participating in video calls, writing a post for the agency's blog—and feeling just as good as I did the day prior to chemo.

Caught up in writing a blog post about employee engagement and culture, I'm pulled out of my zone of concentration by a familiar beeping sound. It's the Neulasta patch. Instead of the ominous wait for the needle prick, this time the beeping alerts me that the medicine to boost my immune system is about to be administered.

"I heard the beeping, babe. No more work today. Come upstairs and relax on the couch," Mark says.

I could have continued working on the blog post. It's not like I was running a marathon. I get up from my desk and walk up the stairs, smiling at how protective Mark is, making sure I follow the doctor's instructions.

I don't feel anything as the medicine goes into my arm. It takes about twenty-five minutes for it to finish. It beeps a final time. Mark sits down next to me and looks at the patch. A green light is illuminated, signaling the reservoir that held the medicine is empty. Mark puts on his reading glasses and refers to the instructions on how to remove the patch from my arm. He lifts the bottom edge and slowly removes the three-inch patch from my arm.

Now, I wait. *How will these cruel drugs affect me?* It's like turning the crank on a Jack-in-the-box, knowing something is going to happen. You keep turning the crank with a looming anticipation. *Will I vomit? I don't want to vomit... that is the worst. Will I lose my sense of taste? Will foods taste like metal?*

The nurses at the infusion center told me to expect the side effects from the Neulasta to begin about two days after the medicine administers. Since my treatment was on Wednesday and the immune system boosting drug administered on Thursday, the side effects should show up on Saturday.

Saturday morning, I wake up feeling achy. The pain isn't too bad. As the day goes on, the pain gets more intense. I've never experienced bone pain before, but that's exactly how it feels. Stronger than a muscle ache. The pain feels like it goes through your muscle and hits your bones. I take Claritin, as the nurses suggested. It helps a little. I spend the day laying on our sectional couch with a heating pad and a blanket. The pain continues through Sunday. I spend another day on the couch with the heating pad. The warmth feels so good, especially on my lower back.

On Monday morning, I wake up and the pain is gone. So, it's back to work. By mid-morning, my stomach doesn't feel very good. I feel a little nauseous. Nausea is a common side effect, so Dr. Al already prescribed Zofran. The small pill dissolves under my tongue. It works fast.

I feel fatigued, too. I'm tired but I notice my body feels so heavy, like someone put a lead vest over my shoulders. It feels like I'm being weighed down. I work for a couple of hours, and then lie down for a bit. After I rest, I bring my laptop to the couch. I'm able to do a little more work. When the fatigue hits again, I put my laptop on the coffee table and rest. I continue this teeter-tottering from work to rest.

A few days later, the gastrointestinal issues set in. They hit in the evening, typically after dinner. After we eat, Mark, the kids, and I converge on the sectional sofa in the family room. I feel a strange rumbling in my lower abdomen. I race to the bathroom. A few minutes later, I rejoin the family, feeling okay again. These short bursts of an upset stomach followed by trips to the bathroom go on for a few agonizing days.

I try to eat bland foods to help with the gastrointestinal side effect. My sense of taste isn't completely gone. It's about thirty percent there. It's so strange to eat a food I've eaten many times before, that I know what it tastes like, but now I can't taste it the same way. I learn that eating certain foods, especially if they're cold, helps. Applesauce and raspberry sorbet are go-to elements of my meals and snacks.

By the end of the second week, the nausea and gastrointestinal issues are gone. My energy returns, too. I actually feel good. Not one-hundred percent good, but a lot better. Then, I remember I have chemo again in a few days.

My office set up in the basement is ideal for working while also recovering from treatment. The majority of the basement is finished. My desk is in the middle of a large open area. Just beyond my desk is a cozy second family room, furnished with two extra couches, a coffee table with dark metal legs and slate tiles, two matching end tables, lamps, and a TV—evidence we merged two households into one. A half bath is at the opposite end of the basement.

My boss is so supportive. She encourages me to take breaks when I need them. She also encourages me to talk with the other members of the team and let them know if I need help. With her support, I don't feel a shred of guilt when I need to rest. Pre-cancer me always felt guilty for taking time off work, even when I was sick. I'd still check and respond to emails throughout the day. I couldn't disconnect and take time for myself. Now, I put my body first.

chapter seven

Day fourteen. I wake to thoughts of losing my hair. *What had been feelings of worry have turned to dread. I look in the mirror and stare at my hair. Tomorrow is day fifteen. I think of the way Mom gave up her hair; the way she did it on her own terms. I step into the house and walk down the hallway toward their living room. Mom sits on the couch. I see her legs, but the rest of her is blocked by a large lamp on the end table. As I get closer to her, she comes into full view. She is dressed in a comfortable looking knit outfit with a white shirt, navy-blue pants, and a cardigan. Her nails look like she's had a fresh manicure—painted a beautiful shade of pink-orange. Her head is covered with the cutest blue and white printed head covering. I try to hide my surprise. When I last saw her, her hair had just started thinning. Aware that I'm looking at the head covering, Mom tells me her hairstylist came to the house and shaved her head a few days ago.*

"Do you want to see what my head looks like?" Mom asks.

"Sure," I say in as lighthearted a manner as I can muster.

Mom tugs at the top of the head covering and it slips off, revealing her bald head. I try not to show how shocked I am. Without hair, she looks so weak and frail... like a cancer patient.

Thoughts of losing my hair consume me for several minutes. I step back from the mirror and turn toward the shower. I want to wash my hair. It's been a couple of days since I washed it, and it feels gross. I'm terrified, though. *What will happen when the water falls onto my hair? Or when I start to shampoo it? Will it start falling out?* I know I technically have one more day, but it's not like that day is set in stone. It was an estimation from Dr. Al. It could be today. It could be a few days away.

I take a deep breath and step into the shower. I stand still for several seconds, letting the warm water fall onto my body. The warmth envelopes me like a comforting blanket. I turn toward the corner shelf that holds our shampoo, conditioner, and soap. My hand shakes as I reach for the shampoo bottle. I pour a small amount of shampoo into my left palm. I stare at the white glob, stalling.

Rubbing my hands together to create a lather, I reach up to the top of my head. I work the shampoo into my hair. I stop for a second and look at my hands. There is more hair than usual on my hands but it's not coming out in clumps. With a sigh of relief, I continue gently massaging the shampoo into my hair. Standing under the shower head, I let the water fall onto my hair. Once the shampoo has rinsed from my hair, I grab my hair as if I was putting it into a ponytail and wring out the water.

I feel a web of strands of hair in my hand. It doesn't feel horrible, but there's certainly a lot more hair tangled around my fingers than I'm used to. Stunned, I look at my hand and the collection of hair in my palm. As I let the hair fall toward the drain, a rush of sadness engulfs me. I start to cry. I reach for my towel that's hung over the glass shower door and bury my face in the towel. I scream into the towel.

AAAAAAAHHHHHHH!

My scream is muffled. I don't want Mark or the kids to hear me. I don't want them rushing into the bathroom to find out what's wrong. I need to feel these feelings on my own. I let myself scream into the towel again. Then, I turn back to the shower head and let the warm water wash away my tears.

Even though I know I am going to lose my hair, I am not ready to shave it off. I don't know why, but I need to take this in steps. Perhaps it's an attempt to gain some control over this cruel side effect of chemo.

My first baby step: contact my hairstylist, Claire, to see if she has time to cut my hair short. Maybe if it's shorter, it won't be as traumatic when it falls out in bigger clumps. I text Claire to see if she can help me. She responds right away.

Hi, Emily! I would be honored to help you with this and cut your hair shorter. One of my clients had to cancel an appointment, so I have an opening tomorrow at 7pm. Will that work for you?

I respond, saying that I'll see her then. With that, I feel a little sense of ease knowing I created a plan for my hair. I'll decide when I'm ready to shave it off.

Instead of straightening my hair, as I've been doing for a few years, I style my hair curly. No need to pull at my hair. As I finish drying my hair with a diffuser, I look at my headful of curls. The curly hair looks really good! When I used to wear my hair curly, one side of my hair would look great, lots of curls. The other side might have some curls with other hair that was partly curly or frizzy. That's why I opted to wear it straight. Of course, my hair decides to cooperate and look really good when I'm about to get it cut short... and then shaved off. Of course it does.

Day fifteen.

I ask Mark to come with me to my hair appointment. While Mark drives, I sit in the passenger seat and stare out the window. My mind is taking me back to the moment in the shower when I wrung water out of my hair and had a lot more hair in my hand than usual. I know losing my hair comes with the territory for cancer treatment. I want to beat cancer. It's just that losing my hair makes me incredibly sad. Except for when I wear a wig, I will look like a cancer patient.

When we get to the salon, Claire walks out to the lobby area to greet us. As she guides us back to her chair, I'm surprised to see how many people are in the salon—some getting their hair cut while others are getting color applied to their hair and others are getting manicures or pedicures.

Claire asks how I've been feeling and asks questions about my treatment. Conversation turns to my hair.

"So, you want to go shorter, maybe a pixie cut?" she asks.

"Yes, that's what I'm thinking. I feel like I need to take a gradual approach to this." I'm nervous. I'm sure it shows.

"That's completely understandable," she adds.

"But, at the same time," I pause, and Claire is patient with me, "I feel like I'm just delaying the inevitable. Should I just shave it now?" I turn to meet Claire's eyes.

"That's completely up to you," she says. "If you feel more comfortable easing into this, that's okay, and that's what you should do. This is your journey. You do whatever feels right to you."

I decide to ease into this and get my hair cut short. Claire spins the chair so that I'm facing the mirror. I look at myself and my hair. Claire puts a black cape over me and snaps it closed at the back of my neck. She grabs a brush and looks at me in the mirror.

"Are you ready?" Claire gently smiles.

"No, but it's out of my control."

"I disagree. You are taking control right now. You are choosing what you want to do with your hair given the situation," she says. I shake my head and agree. "Okay, I'm going to start by brushing through your hair. A lot of hair will probably come out. Look down if you want to."

I try to look away, but it's hard not to look. As Claire brushes through my hair, I'm amazed at how much hair is coming out. Each time Claire runs the brush through the length of my hair, she holds the brush behind the chair, so I don't see it. It looks like she pulls the hair out of the brush and lets it fall to the floor.

I look in the mirror and see a woman in the row of chairs behind me looking over to see Claire brush through my hair and let clumps of hair fall on the floor.

I sit as still as stone. I stare at the narrow table that sits just below her mirror. I hate this so much. I am humiliated. It's like I don't have control over my body. Tears well in the corner of my eye.

Claire puts a hand on my shoulder. "Let's go get you shampooed."

I follow Claire to the small room with chairs and wash basins. I sit down and lay my head back. Claire turns on the water and lets it warm up. I feel the warm water on my head. It feels so nice.

Claire shampoos my hair and massages my scalp. "Hopefully, we were able to brush out any hair that had already fallen out but got tangled in your hair, and you won't lose too much more tonight. It should fall out gradually." *Gradually.* I let myself relax and enjoy the soothing sensations. For a few glorious minutes, I forget that I just lost a bunch of hair. It feels so nice. I would let her do a scalp massage all evening! She rinses out the shampoo and works conditioner into my hair. Once the conditioner is rinsed out, Claire gently wrings the water out of my hair and wraps my hair in a towel.

We walk back to her chair. I sit down and look at myself in the mirror. I'm amazed how much hair I still have! I almost expected to see bald spots. It's definitely thinned out, though. As Claire grabs her scissors, I keep my head still, but drop my eyes so I can't see her cutting several inches off my hair.

It is excruciating. Trying not to watch as something that is such an outward sign of who I am be taken from me. As much as I tell myself this is temporary and that my hair will grow back, it's just such a shitty part of the journey in beating cancer. I want to tell myself, You've got this, but I can't. I'm sad. I let myself feel sad.

Claire finishes cutting my hair. "I know you don't want any of this to be happening, but I have to tell you, this short haircut looks really cute on you."

After a second, I muster the courage to look at myself in the mirror. With tears in my eyes, I look up. I guess it doesn't look too bad.

"Thank you, Claire. I really appreciate you doing this for me."

She brushes little hairs off my neck and removes the black cape. I step out of the chair and take a deep breath. I look in the mirror again. The short curls do remind me of when I was younger. I always wanted to have long hair. Mom wasn't sure how to handle my brunette curls, so she had me keep it short. I never liked the short hair. Almost all my friends had long hair. Their moms would style it in pig tails or a ponytail. As short as my hair was, I couldn't do anything with it.

For now, I'm glad I opted for a short haircut before buzzing it off. I'm not quite ready for that.

Come on, girl. You've got this.

When Mark and I get home, Emma and Stella are sitting on the couch, watching TV. They both run into the kitchen to see my haircut.

"Oh my gosh, Mom! It looks so cute," Stella exclaims.

"It is cute, Mom. You look good with short hair," Emma adds.

"Thank you, girls. You are so sweet."

It's been a traumatic couple of days. Even though it's still a little early, I kiss Mark goodnight. "I guess Dr. Al was right on the mark with his prediction of fifteen days," he says.

I let out a half-hearted chuckle. "Yes, I guess he was."

I am tired in every way a person can be tired, so I let sleep take me over.

***

Working from home has many advantages. One of them is the ultra-casual "dress code," especially when there aren't any client calls on the calendar. My "uniform" of late has been leggings and a sweatshirt or jacket.

My schedule is pretty light, only a couple of video calls with other members of the team. I didn't tell any of my coworkers that I was going to get my hair cut short. I feel self-conscious. It seems silly to be self-conscious about it, especially around coworkers who I've known for many years, but I can't help it. A few minutes before my first video call, I log on. Before I click the "Join" button, I look at myself on the video preview. With the black hood of my jacket against my neck, it's hard to tell that my hair is short. It looks like I have my hair in a clip. Maybe with the hoodie, my short hair won't draw any attention. Not sure why I'm concerned about having my hair short now. It's going to be gone soon!

On a video call a few days later, a coworker noticed my hair and commented that I have a face for short hair. I totally disagree but thank them anyway.

In the shower, I notice more hair falling out. It's not as traumatic as it was a week ago. The shorter length of my hair helps. After towel drying my hair, I work a comb through it. I lean forward toward the mirror to get a closer look. It's getting so much thinner. I can see my scalp in a few areas.

Along with some bald spots, my scalp is incredibly itchy. It's time. I'm ready to shave it off.

After dinner, Mark, the kids, and I are sitting on the couch, watching a rerun of Big Bang Theory. I've seen this episode a few times before. Still, the show makes me laugh out loud. It's good to laugh and take my mind off cancer, chemo, and this vicious side effect... this hair loss.

During a commercial, I share my decision with the family.

"It's time to buzz it off. It's getting so thin and my scalp itches so much. I'm going to call Claire to see if she can do it in the next day or so."

"I noticed it was getting kind of thin, but I didn't want to say anything. I didn't want you to feel bad. You're already upset about losing your hair," Emma says carefully.

"It's okay. I needed to take this in phases." I give her a small smile and a reassuring nod.

"I'll do it for you," Steven says.

I look over at him. "You want to shave my head?" I ask. "You don't have to do that. That's a lot for you, emotionally I mean."

"No, I want to. Are you ready now? I can go get my clippers?" Steven stands up off the couch, already turning to get the clippers. I think about the little boy who lost his dad as I look at Steven. And then I think about the incredible man he's become.

I look at him for a moment longer. I trust him. I trust my family. "Okay. Let's do it," I say. There's no need to wait any longer. It's coming out anyway.

I'm in control of this, chemo. I'm deciding to shave it.

While Steven goes upstairs to get his clippers, I grab a couple of towels and sit on the floor.

Steven stops at the sight of me. "What are you doing on the floor? You can sit on the stool by your sink."

I shake my head no. "I don't want to watch you shave it. I may be deciding to do it, I just don't need to watch!"

Steven shakes his head with resolve. He grabs the clippers in his right hand. I can see them out of the corner of my eye. They look small. I ask Steven if the clippers can do the job.

"Technically, it's a beard trimmer, but I think it will work." We both laugh. I mean, it's not like he can mess it up. The hair is coming out!

He turns on the trimmer. I jump at the sound. I take a deep breath.

I hate this. I fucking hate this.

Since it's a small trimmer, it takes a while to shave all the hair. I sit still. Wanting this to be done. I'm sick of all the emotional energy I put into losing my hair.

Steven turns off the trimmer. It's done. I feel a sense of relief wash over me. I reach my right hand up to touch my head. It's soft with a few areas of stubble. Okay, it's time to face the music. I need to look. I stand on the towel and walk to the mirror to get a closer look. In my mind, I see Mom smile at me, her bald head wrapped in that beautiful blue scarf.

Surprisingly, it doesn't look so bad. I mean, it's not a look I want to go for in the future, but it's okay.

As I walk to the door, I stop to take one more look in the mirror. *You've got this. You're going to beat cancer. You are the storm.*

chapter eight

My second round of chemo is scheduled for December 22nd. Even though this Christmas is plagued by the two C's—cancer and Covid—I don't want to feel crappy around Christmas. Not like this will be a normal Christmas. Even if cancer wasn't in the picture, Covid prevents us from traveling to see family or having family gatherings at our house. Dad will still come over. I call Dr. Al's office to see if it would be a problem to push that appointment out a week. The nurse talks with Dr. Al and gives me the thumbs up to move chemo to December 30th.

We didn't go overboard decorating the house for Christmas. Our tree, with white lights and wild mix of ornaments—from crafts made at daycare and symbols of things the kids liked when they were younger, to treasured cardinal ornaments and beautiful glass ornaments, a football with the Cleveland Browns logo, Brutus Buckeye, and intricate wooden ornaments Mark's dad made. It's a beautiful pastiche of past and present. Our stockings are hung on the mantle. My favorite snow people, Mrs. Snowman and Mr.

Snowman, a wedding present for me and Steve, are on the mantle, too. Many evenings, Mark, the kids, and I watch a TV show or movie by the light of the Christmas tree. It casts a soft, golden glow in the family room. The light and being surrounded by my family fill me with comfort and a sense of peace. I love this time when we're together.

Mark and I are awake before the kids on Christmas morning. Now that they're teenagers, they aren't the ones waking us up at 6am! I turn on the tree lights, make a cup of tea, and snuggle under a blanket on the couch. While it's quiet, I reflect on the past few weeks. I made it through my first round of chemo. I dealt with bone pain, fatigue, nausea, diarrhea, losing my hair, losing some of my sense of taste, and navigating a whole new diet.

Thinking back about the side effects that I experienced, I'm envious of Mom. Even though one of our chemo drugs, Carboplatin, was the same, it seemed like Mom fared far better than me. *Mom was fatigued for a couple of days after chemo, and she had trouble tasting foods and drinks, but things were a bit easier now that she was finally in the rehab facility after the many weeks she spent at the Cleveland Clinic. Mom asked if I could bring her a lemonade. She thought having a little tart flavor might help.*

I stop at the grocery store to buy lemonade. As I scan the options—regular, light, raspberry, strawberry—I pick several options for her to try. Some claim to be more tart, and others are supposed to be sweeter.

I walk into Mom's sterile-looking room at the rehab facility.

"Hi, Mom! I brought a few different lemonades for you to try. I thought we could do a taste test."

I get a plastic cup from her bathroom and pour a small amount of the first lemonade, one claiming to be tart, and hand her the cup. She takes a sip and makes a face. Her scrunched-up face reminds me of videos you see of babies that try a lemon for the first time! We laugh. I pour out what's left of the first one and try the next. This is a raspberry lemonade. Nope. She sneers. We repeat this process a few times until we get to the last one. I saved the strawberry lemonade for last. She takes a sip and smiles.

"This tastes good," she says. I raise my hands victoriously, like I achieved some big feat. I promise to buy more of the strawberry lemonade so she can keep up her fluid intake.

Some change in her taste, low appetite, fatigue, and hair loss seemed to be the extent of Mom's side effects. Those are crappy side effects, but it just wasn't as many or as harsh as mine. Maybe she felt worse but never let on. I wasn't with her 24/7. It seemed like the side effects weren't too hard on her.

I'm on the other side of it, at least the first round, and feel really good now. *You got through it. You can get through the next rounds of chemo because you are the storm.*

Hearing footsteps on the stairs ends my little self-reflection and pep talk session. Emma and Stella walk into the family room wearing the red and black checked pajamas we gave them last night. Since the kids were little, I let them open a gift on Christmas Eve. The present is always a new pair of pajamas. This year, all three kids got the same pattern. Each year on Christmas Eve, one of the kids will ask me if they still get to open that one present before they go to bed!

About an hour later, Steven comes down the stairs wearing his red and black check pajamas. With everyone awake, it's present time. Steven plays Santa, handing out the presents that are overflowing from the bottom of the tree. Since this is how we open presents every year, it feels normal. This year, normal is a very good thing. He also plucks the full stockings from their hooks on the mantle and delivers them to their rightful owner. As I watch the girls pull gifts from their stockings, I'm overcome with gratitude for my dear friend, Martha. Knowing I probably wouldn't feel up to running last minute errands for stocking stuffers, she offered to pick out gifts for the kids' and Mark's stocking.

Later that afternoon, Dad comes over. It feels like our regular Sunday dinners rather than Christmas. Usually, the house is filled with other people—aunts, uncles, my brother and his family, and Mark's side of the family. Regardless, I'm glad my dad feels comfortable coming over to our house. Covid isn't keeping him completely shut in his house.

Dad hated living alone. He often talked about how much he hated cooking for himself and eating alone. He came over to our house a couple evenings a week. I know how lonely he was. I understood that loneliness. *Eventually, Dad contacted someone an independent living facility to schedule a tour. About a week before the date of the tour, Dad asked if I would go with him. It was a beautiful facility, and I could tell dad was very pleased. As we walked to the car, I looked down to see the shape of a heart in the snow. I knew Mom was looking down on us then. Steve, too. I think about them both now, at Christmas dinner, looking at Dad and my children around the table.*

We enjoy a nice dinner together and watch a Christmas movie. I'm grateful to Dr. Al for allowing me to delay my chemo by a week. It's nice to enjoy our small, quiet Christmas without feeling bad.

Treatment number two falls right before New Year's Eve. It's never been a huge holiday for me or for us as a family, so I don't care that I'll be dealing with the effects of chemo. I have to do it anyway. Since I've been through one round, I feel prepared going into the second. Knowing what to expect makes such a big difference.

The only change from first chemo to the second is that I've lost my hair. Along with the wigs, I bought several cotton head coverings in a variety of colors and some headbands. I picked a light blue one to go with my blue flannel shirt and jeans. After we arrive at the hospital and check in, my first stop is to get blood drawn from my port. Next, I see Dr. Al.

Dr. Al knocks on the door of the exam room. "Hello, Emily and Mark. I see you've lost your hair." Just like that.

I bobbed my head up and down. Cancer makes you blunt. "You were right on when you said it would be fifteen days. I started to lose some on day fourteen, but it really came out on the next day."

"I'm sorry that you have to deal with that. Unfortunately, the chemotherapy attacks fast growing cells. Cancer cells grow fast, as do cells in our GI tract, hair, and nails." Dr. Al explains and then comments, "You've coordinated your scarf with your shirt. Was that on purpose?"

"Of course it was! I've got to keep it stylish," I say with a laugh.

We spend time talking about side effects from the first round. I relay my experience, beginning with the bone pain, then upset stomach, GI issues, fatigue, and so on. He reassures me that all of the side effects I mentioned were completely normal. We discuss over-the-counter medicines I've used to help ease the side effects, especially with the GI issues. They've been more difficult to manage. Dr. Al suggests a prescription medicine that could help.

After we leave the exam room, we take the elevator upstairs to the infusion center. A nurse greets us and guides us back to the treatment cubby. She says that once the chemo meds come up from the pharmacy, she can get them started. Since I didn't have any reaction to the medicines being administered on their own for the first round, she'll run two of the medicines together. Instead of being at the infusion center for five and a half hours, we'll be here about four hours.

While we wait for the medicines, I get comfortable in the recliner and unpack some things from my bag that will help pass the time: my iPad and People magazine. I'll watch some shows on Netflix and catch up on celebrity gossip. That will definitely pass the time! The nurse brings the pre-meds, one is an anti-nausea, and the other is a steroid.

About fifteen minutes later, the nurse returns with an IV bag. She calls over another nurse to confirm I'm getting the right medicine at the right dose. After the medicine is double checked, the nurse hangs the IV bag on the pole and connects the line to my port. Round two is on.

The rest of our time at the infusion center unfolds like it did the first time—Taxotere runs first, followed by Carboplatin. This time, Herceptin and Perjeta run simultaneously. Once the medicines are done, the nurse hangs an IV bag with saline. After the saline has run for about twenty minutes, the nurse returns to set up the Neulasta patch.

As I go about the days after the second round of treatment, I realize the side effects, from chemo and the immune-boosting drug, unfold like clockwork. They run the same course. The exact same course. Fatigue. Bone pain. Nausea. Diarrhea. Fatigue. Sense of taste fades. It's like the side effects were on some freaky schedule. A schedule that was strangely and extraordinarily accurate.

It's been about ten months since we first heard the term *Covid-19*. Businesses and restaurants have been forced to close. People are required to work from home. Schools are closed and classrooms have become virtual. Once businesses are allowed to re-open, life resumes with some constraints. Vaccines. Social distancing. Masking. The vaccine and masks, meant to prevent the spread of illness, became contentious.

A few days before my next round of chemo, my phone rings and I see it's from Dr. Al's office. I answer right away.

"Hi, Emily. For your chemo appointment on Wednesday, I need to let you know about an immediate change to our visitor policy. You won't be able to bring a visitor with you to the infusion center," the receptionist says.

I understand we're in the midst of a pandemic. Recommendations and policies are ever-changing. "Really? Why the change?" I ask.

"We've had some issues recently with visitors refusing to wear masks. The nurses have been reminding patients and visitors to put their masks on when they're moving about the infusion center. Some refused to comply. Security had to be called in some instances," she explains.

Unbelievable yet totally believable. People are being so stupid. I share the news with Mark.

"Are you serious?" he asks, visibly irritated. "We wear our masks. We do what we're supposed to. And I can't be there with you?"

I understand why Mark is upset. He wants to be there to support me, but it is what it is. Why get all worked up and upset about it when we can't do anything to change it? I wish Mark could be there with me, but he can't.

With my iPad charged and magazines in my bag, I'll have plenty of things to occupy my time.

At the third round of chemo, I'm beginning to feel like a pro. I know what to expect. And because two of the drugs can run simultaneously, the span of treatment doesn't last as long. The most disappointing aspect of this round is that Mark can't be here with me.

Before grabbing my iPad to binge Schitt's Creek on Netflix, I check my work email on my phone. My boss sent me a note. The subject line reads, "Interested in presenting at the NAHC conference?" I open the email right away. She asks if I would be interested in co-presenting a talk during a session as part of a virtual conference for a national healthcare association. Immediately, I'm struck by the duality of my reaction. On the one hand, I'm proud and excited about the opportunity to give a presentation for a conference with healthcare leaders across the country. Then, there's the obvious. I am going through chemo. I'm fearful about not just giving the presentation, but creating the presentation along with my co-worker, rehearsing it and feeling ready to give the presentation virtually. I look up at the IV pole and see two bags of chemo drugs flowing into me.

Will I be able to get through a presentation? Can I do it well? This is a big deal.

My first thought is that I can't do it. It's a great opportunity, it's important to my career, but I just can't do everything. *Plus,* I remind myself, *you're also going through chemo. Like, in this moment, you are getting chemo.*

The conference is a little less than two months away. I'll still be going through chemo at the end of February. I'm not sure how to respond to my boss's request. To help me decide, I look at the date of the presentation and pull up my calendar to map out when it will take place in my chemo schedule. The conference falls on the third week of one of my rounds of chemo. That's my good week.

It's odd, yet there's no question as to how I'll feel from the time chemo ends until the next treatment. A peculiar routine that's oddly helpful as I continue at my job as an account lead at the marketing agency, especially as I contemplate co-presenting at this conference.

I can do this. I've got a wig. It will happen during my good week. So, I respond to her email, agreeing to be a co-presenter for the conference session.

It feels more than a little crazy, but I'm going to do it. My client work is a bit light right now. I can put in the time to work on the presentation. And it's a topic I know well: employee engagement.

There is one concern I have. It's a new side effect that eludes the bizarre routine of the other side effects. Watery eyes. My eyes water constantly. I am a makeup girl. I wear makeup every day. The unending trickle of water from my eyes is maddening. Waterproof mascara is useless. Tissues are with me wherever I go. A box of tissues is on my desk. A tissue lays just to the right of my laptop—close enough for me to grab and dab at my eyes countless times during the day. A wad of clean tissues is in my purse and my chemo bag. I'll have to figure out how I can dab at my eyes during the presentation. Late February is too early to blame it on allergies! I'll figure it out.

One of the first times my eyes started watering was when I was on a video call with my coworkers. I saw concerned looks on their faces.

"Don't worry, I'm not crying! My eyes will not stop watering. It's just one of the exasperating side effects of chemo," I wave my hands and motion for them to proceed with the meeting, hoping they'll ignore me constantly wiping my eyes.

I find it so vexing because it's always there. Other side effects come and go. Bone pain, stomach aches, and intestinal issues linger for a while. Fatigue happens just a few days after treatment. My sense of taste comes and goes. But the watery eyes are aggravating. I complain about it all the time.

Like the side effects, my appointments with Dr. Al followed by the chemo treatments fall into a routine. Blood draw. Step on the scale. Appointment with Dr. Al. Chemo. Only now, there's another visible side effect.

As I get dressed for my appointment, I put on a pair of dark blue skinny jeans and a button-down flannel shirt. The jeans, which used to fit rather snuggly, are a bit big in the waist. I grab a belt, so I won't have to keep pulling them up. After I thread the black belt through the loops on the waist of the jeans, I connect the two metal ends. I laugh to myself as the belt, fastened as tight as I can get it, hangs off my waist.

At the visit for my sixth and final round of treatment, Dr. Al casually asks, "Did we talk about the possibility of chemo putting you into menopause?"

"Ah, what? No, you did not tell me this! That is absolutely something I would remember. What do you mean I could go into menopause?" I felt blindsided, and it read all over my face.

I'm dumbfounded by this. Menopause isn't even on my radar. It seemed like it was still many years away. I'm forty-seven. Mom didn't go into menopause until her fifties. My mind is spinning. I don't know what to say.

He explains that chemo suppresses the functioning of the ovaries. Dr. Al goes on to drop this statistic on me using an analogy—a car analogy at that.

"Younger women, say in their thirties, have a good chance that their ovaries will rev back up and they'll resume having normal cycles. For women in their forties, like you, well, there's an eighty percent chance your ovaries won't rev back up."

"Are you serious?" It seems as if he's being a little too lighthearted about this. Menopause. That's a big deal. I don't really know much about menopause. I remember Mom complaining of hot flashes and her period being irregular. That's it. That's all I know. And I can't ask Mom about it.

He goes on to say, "If after a couple of months your cycle does not return, we will consider that you've gone into what's called 'medical menopause.'"

I'm not even sure how to react to this. I've come to expect what will happen after each round of treatment, down to the day. But this?

I never thought about menopause in relation to cancer. This feels big. I don't know what to think about it. And I can't really put much thought into it. I'm finishing chemo. Next, while I'm dealing with the side effects, I need to make the mental shift to prepare for surgery. *This is too much.*

He goes on to drop another bomb. He says there won't be a gradual entry into menopause. I'm just going to be dropped into the deep end of the menopause pool.

But Dr. Al doesn't know I've been dropped into the deep end before.

chapter nine

I have never dreaded a single day more in my life. Randy, Steve's dear friend, drove me to the funeral home for the visitation. Driving up the two-lane road into Oak Harbor, I felt numb. I didn't know what to think. I just sat there, feeling empty, like a shell. As we pulled into the parking lot, I felt a knot in the pit in my stomach. How was this happening? How am I supposed to stand there as family, friends, coworkers, and acquaintances come in. What do I say?

Walking through the door, I'm overpowered by the scent of lilies. I see so many beautiful floral arrangements scattered around the room. Out of the corner of my eye, I see Steve lying in a casket. I feel lightheaded and sick to my stomach. I don't want to do this. The funeral director, Chris, greets me.

I take a deep breath. I don't have a choice. I have to do this.

As people start to come in, I take my place off the edge of the casket. People who knew Steve introduce themselves to me. They look lost, like they're in disbelief. Same. Some say they're sorry, that they don't know what to say. Same.

golden scars

My cousin Ally comes up next to me. I tell her I feel lightheaded. My mom can tell I don't feel well. They both whisk me back to the kitchen area. Trays of food and cookies line the counter. I take a seat on the couch and put my head between my knees. How is this happening? I can't shake that question.

I try to eat some crackers. While I'm sitting there, I hear familiar voices in the hallway. Friends I used to work with are looking for me. I hear my mom say that I'm not feeling well. I join my mom to say hello to her friend Karen. She says how sorry she is and offers to help. She says she'd provide free grief counseling sessions for me and the kids. I thank her for the kind offer and tell her I will take her up on it.

I worry about Stevie. He just turned eight. He could tell something was wrong with his dad. On the day of his birthday party, Stevie asked me if his dad was feeling okay and if he'd be at the party. I assured him that his dad would be there.

We decided to have Stevie's birthday party at the natatorium at the high school. Stevie and his friends could swim, and we'd have pizza and cake. If you didn't know it, you wouldn't have thought anything was wrong with Steve. He was like a big kid jumping into the pool with the other kids. The kids laughed at Steve as did a cannonball, splashing water on Stevie and his friends. I remember hearing one of the kids tell Stevie that his dad was so cool. It was so good to see Steve having fun. He had been so down for weeks now.

Stevie had a ball at his party.

I never would have imagined that just two weeks later we'd be in a funeral home, with Steve lying in a casket.

It was both brutal and manageable. It was grueling, but I got through it. Chemo is done! I lost my hair, food didn't taste the best, my ankles are swollen, and there were days I didn't feel well, but all of that is behind me.

While some side effects may linger a little longer, Dr. Al has assured me they are short term and will go away with time as my body heals.

As we wait in the now very familiar exam room at Dr. Al's office, I feel such a great sense of accomplishment. I got through what has been deemed the harshest part of my treatment. A rush of happiness and pride courses through me.

There's a knock at the door and Dr. Al steps into the exam room with a smile and says, "You did it! Congratulations. I know that wasn't easy for you."

I admit that I feel incredibly proud of myself. I didn't know what I was facing. Even though he and the team of nurses could tell me what it would be like, chemo is incomprehensible until you go through it. There isn't any way to truly prepare yourself for something like that. But I knew it was key to beating breast cancer.

Dr. Al asks if he can do a breast exam to see if the tumor has decreased in size. I walk over to the exam table and sit down. I move my bra out of the way. He feels around the base of my right breast, the spot where the tumor is. He feels along both sides and back to the bottom. He sits back and looks me in the eye. After a few seconds, he smiles and says, "I don't feel any evidence of the tumor."

"You don't? The cancer is gone!" I exclaim.

"We will need to do an MRI to be sure, but I cannot feel any mass," Dr. Al says.

It was hard to contain my excitement. The chemo worked! As hard as it was, it did its job. Some of the lingering side effects that have been more annoying than anything else—swollen ankles and watery eyes—are overshadowed by total and complete exhilaration.

The chemo worked! The tumor is gone.

"So, does this mean I still have to have surgery?" I ask. Part of me is kidding, but there's a part of me that is serious, too.

"Remember, to get to the 95% cure rate, you need to complete chemo, surgery, and the immunotherapy with anti-cancer infusions. Yes, surgery is the next step," Dr. Al says. He is not kidding at all.

Surgery hasn't even taken a nanosecond of thought up to this point. I have been laser-focused on getting through chemo. It's like I had to compartmentalize chemo. My mind wasn't able to even grasp the idea of surgery or the two options I have for the second phase of treatment.

Now, I have to make the mental shift from celebrating the end of chemo, and possibly the obliteration of the tumor, to the next phase of treatment.

The next step.

When Karen offered free grief counseling sessions, I knew I wanted to take Stevie. He was aware something was up with his dad. The poor kid was just eight. I worried that if I didn't handle this right, it could easily send Stevie down a bad path. I feel an immense responsibility to take care of Stevie, and the girls, too. The girls are so young, just four and a half.

When I call to schedule a time to bring Stevie in to talk with Karen, Karen says she feels like we need to work toward telling Stevie everything, including how his dad died. I say no, immediately. He's eight years old and he just lost his dad unexpectedly. I am not ready to broach the subject of suicide with my son. Karen pushes the issue a bit more, but I push back harder. No, I am not ready to go there. Not now. Right now, I just want to get a sense of what Stevie's thinking, what he's worrying about, and how I can help him through the grief. At the end of our conversation, it sounds as if she is in agreement—we won't go down the path of how Steve died.

Driving to the counseling session, I tell Stevie that we're just going to talk with Karen about dad, what it means to grieve, talk about our feelings—as much as he wants to, and then decide if we want to keep talking with Karen. I'm not sure how the session will go. Stevie does not open up easily. He's quiet. He keeps things bottled up, and he may not open up to her.

When we arrive at Karen's office, we are greeted by the cutest, small dog with curly hair named Mr. Bojangles. I look over at Stevie to see him smiling ear to ear. With that, I can feel some of the nervousness disappear.

Karen guides us into a room with two oversized chairs facing one another. Stevie and I sit in one of the chairs and Karen sits in the chair opposite us. Charlie jumps right into Stevie's lap. To start the session, Karen asks Stevie some questions: school, sports, friends, and so on. Then, she eases in with a few questions about Steve. She kindly tells Stevie how sorry she is that his dad died. She also says she wants to help him understand the feelings he may have and ways to help him deal with them, especially when he feels sad or angry.

The conversation seems to be going well. I can tell Stevie is a bit guarded, but he is responding to Karen's questions.

Then, she asks a question that infuriates me. "Stevie, do you know where your dad was when he died?"

What in the hell? We weren't going to go there. I was not prepared to go there, and I knew Stevie wasn't ready.

I could sense Stevie tensing up. I try to get Karen's attention without Stevie realizing I am furious. Stevie shakes his head no.

If that isn't enough, Karen presses further. "Do you want to know where your dad was when he died?"

I am livid. I try again to get her attention, but Karen will not take her eyes off Stevie. Stevie shakes his head no. I look over at him, and he looks terrified.

I couldn't believe Karen approached this first session that way. I'm not a grief counselor, but it seems so brash and unsympathetic.

Karen can tell Stevie is shutting down. He is done talking to her. She asks Stevie if he'd like to do some art. He says yes, so we walk over to the art area while Karen explains how art can be a great way for kids to express how they're feeling. He has the option to paint, color, or mold clay. He chooses to paint.

Stevie takes a piece of paper and selects some paint colors. He picks up a brush and dabs it into the red paint. He puts the paintbrush on the paper and begins making big circles with the paint. He puts some force into his brushstrokes. In no time, the paper is nearly covered in red paint.

"He's angry," I think. I walk over to Karen and whispered that to her. All she does is nod her head yes.

After Stevie finishes painting, Karen thanks him for coming and says she hopes he comes back to talk to her again.

In my mind, I think, "Hell no." If this is how she handles grief counseling with kids, it's not for us.

She broke the trust I felt following our initial conversation about not telling Stevie everything. By her asking if Stevie knew where Steve was when he died, we'd have to go into more detail about why he was in our garage. And why he was in our garage, sitting in his truck with the garage door closed. I felt betrayed. I know my children. And I trust myself. In my gut, it did not feel right to tell Stevie the whole story. Not yet.

We walk out the door and head to the car. Before the door closes behind us, Stevie asks me, "So, Mom. Where was dad when he died?"

Son of a bitch. I'm not ready for this. How am I supposed to answer this question without lying to him?

I take a deep breath and try to gather my thoughts. My head is spinning. I am angry at Karen for putting me in this position. As we drive home, I remind Stevie that his dad hadn't been feeling well. I told him that his doctor was trying different medicines to help him feel better. I said that the medicines he was taking could confuse your thinking and mess with your head. Then, I said that his dad planned to stay home from work that day because he hadn't been sleeping well. I said that maybe later that day he felt a little better and wanted to go somewhere, maybe he wanted to go fishing. As we pulled into our driveway, I told Stevie that I found his dad in his truck. I didn't say anymore. I waited to see if Stevie would have any questions. He just said, "Okay, Mom."

I pulled my car into the garage, into the very spot where Steve's truck was. I hated putting my car in the garage, but I didn't want the kids asking me why I wasn't driving into the garage or why I was leaving it on our driveway. So, I drove into the garage every day. And every day, it was like a sucker punch to the stomach.

golden scars

I put the car in park and look up at the wall and the door that leads into the house. The same thing Steve would have been looking at when he was in his truck.

During the breast clinic a few months ago, I was introduced my surgeon. Dr. Cunningham is a well-known and well-respected surgeon in our area. She leads the breast cancer program for the health system where I'm receiving care. I remember hearing her name when I worked there.

I'm really looking forward to meeting her. Mark and I walk down the long hallway to Dr. Cunningham's office. As we open the door, we step into a small, dimly lit waiting room. I walk up to the desk to check in.

After a few minutes, my name is called. A nurse escorts us to a small exam room. Unlike the sterile feeling of the exam rooms in Dr. Al's office, this room, although a fraction of the size, has a big window. The addition of natural light makes a huge difference. Even though the window looks out on a car dealership, it's nice to have something to look at other than pale walls.

After a few minutes, Dr. Cunningham walks into the room. I estimate she's in her sixties. She has long brown hair that's pulled up into a bun, but some of the hair has slipped out. It's late in the afternoon, and I wonder if the mess of her hair means she spent her morning in surgery with her hair tucked in a surgical cap.

There's a warmth and gentleness about her; a maternalistic feel. I've just met her, but I feel completely at ease with her.

"I understand you may have had a complete pathologic response to the chemotherapy. That's wonderful," she says.

"Yes, I am so happy and very relieved!"

Our conversation quickly shifts to the two options for surgery. Dr. Cunningham explains both options in detail. The first is a lumpectomy. She will remove any traces of the tumor and a small percentage of tissue around what's left of it or where it had been located. This type of surgery is followed by several weeks of radiation.

The second surgery is a mastectomy. It can be unilateral, meaning the side on which I had cancer will be removed, or bilateral, also often called a double mastectomy. In this surgery, all breast tissue is removed. If I opt to have reconstruction, a medical plastic surgeon will take over and the initial steps for reconstruction will happen right away. Spacers will be temporarily implanted. The spacers help to create the area in which my own tissue, taken from other areas of my body, like my stomach or thighs, are formed into implants, or artificial implants are placed. After the skin has sufficient time to stretch, I'd have a second surgery to remove the spacers and have the implants placed.

Given the fact that I don't want the cancer to return, I am opting for the more aggressive route—a double mastectomy. I want reconstruction as well. Much like the wig I had been searching for, I want to look like myself as much as possible.

Since the nurse who led us into the exam room asked me to change into a gown, I figured Dr. Cunningham would want to have a look-see as well. I find myself getting quite used to doctors looking at my chest.

Dr. Cunningham sits beside me and examines my breasts. Like Dr. Al had done, she feels around the base of my right breast and along both sides.

"I don't feel anything," she says. Her tone sounds as if this was the first time she'd examined the chest of a woman without any lumps. She seemed genuinely astounded and excited for me. This has probably happened countless times during the course of her career, yet she makes me feel like this is the first time it has happened for her, too!

Before we set a date for the surgery, she says Mark and I will need to meet with the medical plastic surgeon, Dr. Ponce.

While Dr. Cunningham has a calming presence, Dr. Ponce is like electricity. She's petite with beautiful long, black hair and energy for days.

With the direction for surgery set, Dr. Ponce helps us understand the types of implants. There's the DIEP flap, in which my own tissue would be used to form breast tissue.

Pretty quickly, she says, "You would not be a candidate for that type of reconstruction."

"Why not? I think I have some extra to work with," I say jokingly. I wasn't opposed to the idea of a mastectomy and a little liposuction!

The answer remains, "No."

The other types of implants are saline or gel. My first concern is about safety, especially the gel implants. She assures us that implants have come a long way and the gel implants used for reconstruction post-mastectomy are safe.

She says there is one issue with saline implants. With movement, ripples can be seen under the skin.

"That's got to look weird," I say.

Not that I wear a lot of low-cut tops, but I don't like the idea of it looking like I'm skipping a rock on a puddle under my skin. Maybe it wouldn't be that visible, but I don't want to be self-conscious about it.

I decide on gel implants.

Dr. Ponce wants to take some measurements. I walk toward her, and off comes my top again. While she's moving the tape measure along different points on my chest, my mind drifts.

What will my breasts look like after the surgery? Will the nipple still be there? Will I be able to feel any sensation?

I ask Dr. Ponce about what to expect in terms of the look and aesthetics after surgery. She tells me that since my cancer was at the base of my breast, there is a possibility to spare the nipple. She won't know until I have the breast MRI right before surgery.

The date is set. April 22nd.

The idea of surgery is getting more concrete in my mind. It will be a double mastectomy with gel implants. I'm not too nervous about it, at least at this point. A c-section has been my only other major surgery. I wasn't under general anesthesia, though. I was awake during the whole thing; alert to hear the first cries of my twin girls.

The pandemic has us living in our own little Covid bubbles. People are staying at home, even working from home. Everyone wears masks when they're out in public. It's a strange existence right now for everyone. My existence includes that plus cancer treatment. My trips out of the house are pretty much limited to doctor's appointments, chemo, and sometimes to pick up groceries. I've been given the green light from Dr. Al to get the Covid vaccine. The two-dose vaccine is given four weeks apart.

The morning of surgery, I wake up with a surprisingly calm feeling. I see the sun streaming through the blinds of our bedroom windows. I lay in bed for a few minutes thinking about the past few months of treatment and what's in front of me. The breast MRI confirmed I had a complete pathologic response to the chemo. There's "no evidence of disease."

I feel the sense of gratification and accomplishment rise within me again. I'm so proud of myself. I got through something so difficult. I'm incredibly relieved that the chemo is over, but there's this wild feeling of conquering something that threatened my life. I guess the saying, "What doesn't kill you makes you stronger," is true. The cancer was aggressive and could have grown and spread to other areas without me knowing it. But we caught it early. Chemo did its job. Now, surgery will be the added protection against cancer returning.

Steven, Emma, and Stella are in the family room, waiting for me. I walk out of the bedroom with my bag for the hospital, and I can see the nervous and concerned looks on their faces.

"Guys, it's going to be okay," I say to reassure them. "Remember, the cancer is gone." While I'm feeling good going into the surgery, I look at them and remember how much they've already been through. The weight of that is not lost on me.

I was not alone in my grief. I had three young children who were grieving, too. How do you tell an eight-year-old boy and four-year-old girls that their dad died? I couldn't grasp it myself. How would they understand it? How would I talk with them about their dad being gone? He wasn't just gone on a fishing trip. He was gone.

On difficult days, I hid my grief from the kids. I didn't want them to see me crying. I didn't want them to see me when I broke down. They didn't need to be worried about me. They had enough to deal with. When the kids were occupied watching a movie, I tip-toed upstairs to my room. I left the door open, and I went to my walk-in closet. I fell to the floor and cried. I muffled the sound of my cries so they wouldn't hear me. I had to let it out. I was so sad. Words can't really describe the depth of my sadness. It hurt. But it also physically hurt. It was as if I could feel my heart break again and again.

For some reason, the car became a place where the kids often asked questions about their dad, especially the girls. This was good for me, mainly because they couldn't see my face. The question would come out of left field. Questions could be anything from, "Why did Daddy die?" to, "Did medicines make Daddy die?" or, "What happened to Daddy?"

Often, my eyes got big, and I'd take a deep breath. I had to figure out how to answer the questions in ways they'd understand. I didn't broach the subject of suicide until the kids were much older. Usually, I could get about halfway through my answer, thinking I was doing a great job and that the kids were understanding what I was saying, but then one of the girls would ask a question on a completely different topic or blame the other one for burping or farting. Then came the glorious sound of laughter from the kids! Talk about limited attention span.

At the end of the school year, when the girls were six, they came home from school a bit distraught. Usually, the last day of school is full of excitement. The girls said they were in art class and the assignment was to color pictures for Father's Day. They went up to the teacher and said that they didn't have a dad; their dad was in Heaven. They asked if there was something else they could do. Supposedly, the teacher said, "No."

I can't imagine what the girls were thinking as they sat down to color the pages with pictures of dads, strewn with wishes of a "Happy Father's Day." They were so young.

They gave the drawings to me. I told them that I was sorry they had to color the pictures. I told them I could imagine how hard it was. They said yes, but skipped on through the house celebrating that it was finally summer.

In that moment, I realized that I process situations like this so much more deeply than a six-year-old child is able to. Still, it was shitty for the teacher not to find something else for the girls to do. She could have taken that time to tell the girls how sorry she was that their dad wasn't here. To tell them it would be okay.

I came across those drawings not too long ago. It made me feel sad for the girls and what they may have experienced that day. But I was also reminded of the incredible resilience of children. It was sad, but their little minds couldn't comprehend the magnitude of the loss.

There's a beauty in their ability to stay in the moment, to try to understand something so difficult, but not dwell on it. They shift to something else, something that catches their eye or something they want to do that brings them joy. They don't spiral into a dark place. They don't remain sad. And I knew I couldn't either. I was resilient, too. They reminded me of that.

We get to the hospital at 7:30am. A sweet older woman wearing a blue volunteer jacket sits at the information desk and greets us with a lovely smile. She directs us to take the elevator upstairs to the surgery registration desk. Another patient is checking in. As we wait our turn to check in, I'm aware of how calm I feel. I'm a bit surprised that I'm not uneasy. I thought that I would be a nervous wreck. Sometimes, it seems like the anticipation of something new is fraught with negatives and what ifs. Then worry sets in.

That's just not the case. I am grateful for the calm feeling, the sense of peace. It's as if I'm wrapped in love and good thoughts from family and friends. I feel their prayers. I'm ready.

Before I go back for surgery, the dynamic duo, Dr. Cunningham and Dr. Ponce, come into my room. In her usual calm demeanor, Dr. Cunningham says hello and asks how I'm feeling about the surgery. I tell her I'm ready to take this big step to show cancer that I'm stronger than it.

As she always is, Dr. Ponce is walking sunshine. She brings the energy into the room.

"Today is the day, Emily. No more breast cancer, ever!"

She confirms the plan for surgery one last time: double mastectomy with immediate reconstruction. Then, she and Dr. Cunningham drop some great news... well, potentially great news.

"I am nearly positive we can do the surgery as a skin-sparing, nipple-sparing double mastectomy. That means we can save the outer skin of your breast as well as the nipple. What you'll see will be a scar on the base of your breasts," Dr. Cunningham says.

A sense of liberation washes over me. I kicked cancer's ass with the chemo. Now, my trepidation about what I'll look like after the surgery fades. Obviously, the surgery is about so much more than the vanity, but I can't deny the comfort in knowing that when I see myself in the mirror, the reminders of cancer won't be so glaring. I'll have scars, but the scars won't be ugly. They'll be like inscriptions, signifying this integral part of my life's story.

Dr. Ponce says, "To add to that great news, we may be able to place the implants today and skip the spacers. I won't know for sure until we get to that part of the surgery, but I want you to know there's a good chance this will be a one-and-done surgery."

I don't mind if we have to go the spacer route before the implants. Although I tell her to do what she needs to do in surgery, I quietly hope that we can do this in one surgery. Even the possibility of a one-and-done surgery makes me feel like I've won something, like I stuck it to cancer.

As we're talking, the nurse gives me one of the first drugs that will put me to sleep. I feel relaxed, like I don't have a care in the world… and that's the last thing I remember.

***

I hear a whisper in my ear. "You did it, sweetheart! The surgery is over, and the doctor was able to put the implants in. Only one surgery." Although Mark's voice is just a whisper, I can hear the relief and excitement in it.

It's over.

chapter ten

On the morning of Mom's funeral, our family gathered to say our goodbyes. *As we pull into the parking lot of the funeral home, my heart feels heavy. My body feels numb. I don't know what else to think except that I can't believe this is it—the final time I will see my mom. This isn't how I want to see her, though.*

I open the car door and the rush of cold air feels especially harsh.

Inside, Dad walks up to the casket first. The rest of our family—my brother, his wife and my nephew, Mark and the kids, my aunts, uncles, and I--hold back to give dad some time alone with Mom. His head bows down. Seeing my dad deepens the heaviness in my heart—watching him say goodbye to his wife of fifty years.

Tears begin to well in the corner of my eyes.

I know how he is feeling. I was in that same position ten years ago as I leaned into the casket to say goodbye to Steve.

golden scars

This is different for my dad. My parents were married for so long, raised two children, adored time spent with their four grandchildren. They traveled during their retirement. And in the last year, Dad took care of Mom as she fought so hard to beat cancer.

Mark, the kids, and I approach the casket to say our goodbyes. Mom looks so beautiful. She looks like she is at peace. Although it is gut wrenching to know this is my last goodbye, I know she isn't in pain. Her body is no longer failing her. I hoped she and Steve are there with us, both of them free of the pain they experienced. It feels like a colossal clash of emotions. I'm glad mom is not suffering. I'm devastated she's gone. I hope she's at peace.

I open my eyes and look around the room. I squint as the light seems especially bright. I look to my right to see Mark standing next to the bed rail. I remember him whispering to me that the surgery had gone well. Dr. Ponce was able to place the implants. Surgery was one and done. Phase two of treatment is over.

My head begins to clear from the grogginess of the anesthesia. My thoughts turn to my chest. I'm curious what it looks like. *Do I still have nipples?* Dr. Cunningham said she would need to take a sample of tissue from my right nipple to make sure there wasn't any cancer there. *Will I have any sensation on my skin? How will the incisions look after they heal?*

I look down at my chest and see a white cotton bra that extends below my rib cage and has a zipper on the front. It looks a bit like a sports bra, but a really unattractive hospital version of a sports bra. I see the edges of dark purple bandages peeking out from the top of the bra. I didn't expect the bandages to be so colorful!

I unzip the sports bra to get a better look at the bandages. There are more tubes hanging from me than I expected! The purple bandages covering each breast have tubes that connect to a device that's laying on the bed next to me. It's as big as my hand. I pick up the device. It's heavy. I remember Dr. Ponce saying that she uses special bandages and wound vacs that use negative pressure to promote healing. I turn it over and see there's a clip on the back of it. I guess that means I can go hands-free. Looks like wherever I go, it will be going with me.

If that wasn't enough, I have other tubes hanging from me. The tubes, one on each side, are about three inches below where I assume the incisions are. They're drains to help remove excess fluid from the surgery. The end of the tube connects to a small bulb that collects the fluid.

What a sight I am. I look like a human water sprinkler. I think of the toy water sprinklers from when I was a kid. One was a big green bug that had brightly colored flexible tubes. When the water turned on, the bug started spinning, and the colorful tubes spun around, spraying water. Spin me around and you'd probably get the same effect! I chuckle at the image in my mind.

The nurse comes into my room to teach me how to empty the drains. She hands me a paper with a chart on it. I need to record the amount of fluid in each bulb and then dispose of it appropriately. As I look at the chart, I think how much Steven will geek out on this. As a nursing student, he often asks me or Mark if he can practice taking a blood pressure or listening to our heartbeats. I know he'll want to help out with these drains.

After one night in the hospital, I'm ready to go home.

On the drive home from the hospital, I'm lost in thought about my cancer journey thus far. I finished six rounds of chemo. Surgery is done.

Dr. Cunningham removed three lymph nodes, even though initial testing showed no cancer had spread to the lymph nodes. The final pathology report will be done in a few days. Mark turns down our road and I spot our house. I feel like a warm, comforting blanket has been put on me. It feels so good to be coming home. As he pulls into the driveway and the garage door opens, I know this is the only place I want to be. Home. It's been my cocoon of comfort and healing since I started treatment six months ago. Mark and the kids are here.

As Mark drives the car into the garage, the door from the garage to the house opens and I see Steven, Emma, and Stella crowded into the door frame. They're all smiling, undoubtedly happy to see their mom at home. Because of Covid, they weren't able to visit me at the hospital. Mark kept the kids and my dad updated on the progress of my surgery and when it was over. I know that's not the same. Mark shifts the car into park. I unhook the seatbelt and start to open the car door.

"Hang on. Let me help you. Remember, you just had surgery," Mark says. I'm not in much pain, so it's easy to forget I was just in the hospital and endured an hours-long surgery.

Mark walks to the passenger side of the car and opens the door. I swing my legs out of the car and pick up the hand-held device for the wound vac before I stand up. Even though there's a clip on the back to hook it onto a belt, it's too heavy. I tried to clip it onto the elastic band on my knit pants, but it was so heavy it pulled my pants down. I guess I'll be holding it wherever I go. Mark puts his left hand on the small of my back and guides me up the two stairs into the house.

"Mom! How are you feeling?" Stella asks as she comes toward me and gives me a gentle kiss.

"I'm doing okay. I feel pretty good, just tired. I'm really glad to be home."

Emma and Steven walk up to give me a light hug before going to get my things out of the car and bring them into the house.

Marks asks me if I want to lay down on my bed. I remind him I'm going to make myself comfortable in the recliner that's in our family room.

Before surgery, I turned to social media to prepare for what it would be like after surgery. I was curious to know how the breast cancer survivors I follow recovered. Where did they sleep? What products were helpful to them? Many of the women said they spent several days and nights in reclining chairs. Lying in bed wasn't comfortable for them, even with extra pillows for support.

Mark helps me to create a cozy little nest in the tan leather recliner. It sits in the heart of our home—in the room where we all watch TV and hang out. It's near the steps that lead up to the kids' bedrooms and is also next to the kitchen. I can rest but also be in the hub of activity. I set up the end table next to the recliner with magazines, a book, my phone, iPad, and a water bottle. I also have extra pillows and blankets on the other side of the chair.

I sit in the recliner, and Mark turns the handle to raise the footrest. He lays a soft pink blanket over my legs. I never sit in this chair, but it's really comfortable and provides the right support I need. My pain isn't bad. There's some discomfort, but it's not pain. I take ibuprofen regularly for any discomfort and swelling. I expected to be sorer than I am. I admit my experience with surgeries is limited, though. The only other surgery I had was a c-section when the girls were born. The c-section obviously was more invasive than the mastectomy. Dr. Cunningham didn't have to cut into muscle like my obstetrician did.

Being the student nurse that he is, Steven is interested in checking out all of the tubes I have protruding from my body. He's especially interested in the drains. I show him the form to document the fluid and tell him about emptying the drains throughout the day.

"I'll help you do it," Steven says with the enthusiasm of a student getting real-world practice.

"Hi, Mrs. Zarecki, my name is Steven and I'll be your nurse today," he jokes.

I put down the footrest on the recliner and pick up the device for the wound vac. Steven stands next to the recliner to see if I need help getting up. I walk into the bathroom. Steven grabs an old plastic cup to empty the drains. He holds up the left-side drain to see how much fluid collected in the bulb. After he documents the amount on the form, he unscrews the cap from the bulb and empties the fluid into the plastic cup. As he is about to replace the cap, I show him how to squeeze the bulb to create a small vacuum inside the tube to help draw out the fluid.

I watch as Steven repeats the process on the right-side drain. I can tell he's going to be a great nurse.

"Okay, Mrs. Zarecki, time to get you back to your recliner," he says playfully.

As I get comfortable in the recliner, Steven puts the blanket across my legs. He reaches behind him and acts as if he is getting hand sanitizer from a dispenser. "Can I get you anything before I go? If you need anything, press your call button!"

Emma took over as chef for the family while I was in treatment. She spends time researching recipes on Pinterest and planning out dinner ideas for the week. Now, though, my dear friend Laila has stepped in to make sure the kids and Mark don't have to think about making dinner for a couple of weeks. She organized a meal train with mutual friends and fellow colleagues. Laila sent the meal train link to me so I could see which days meals would be covered. When I look at the schedule, my eyes fill with tears. Two former coworkers, Laura and Angie, both of whom I worked with several years ago but don't know too well, were the first to sign up. Looking at the list of people who said yes to bringing our family dinner fills me with love and gratitude.

Wondering what might be for dinner those nights was fun. One night was a smorgasbord of yummy dishes from a Mediterranean restaurant. Days later, we received an assortment of sandwiches, salads, and flatbreads from Panera. Another night, we enjoyed pulled pork and all the fixings from one of our favorite barbeque restaurants. The next week, we were treated to a homemade breakfast for dinner, or brinner, as we call it.

What probably seems like a small gesture or something easy to do, like sending dinner, left an imprint on my heart that I'll never forget. It's true what they say: the little things really are the big things in life. I can feel so much love around me, even Steve's.

I longed for a sign, something little to let me know Steve was finally at peace. I want to know that the demons he fought were gone. That he was finally free of the depression that had burdened him for so long.

Maybe I was trying too hard to find a sign. Maybe I was closed off to receiving any kind of sign. I was angry that he was gone. I felt abandoned, being left to raise three young children on my own. This was not supposed to be how my life went on, without Steve.

So, I stopped looking for signs. I had so many other things vying for my attention, especially my three young children. I was solely responsible for them. I was solely responsible for keeping a roof over our heads. I was solely responsible for guiding their education, making sure they were doing okay as we all figured out life without Steve.

The first time I felt like I received a sign from Steve was on November 12, 2015. Steve's birthday. The next day would have been our sixteenth wedding anniversary. Five months earlier, on June 20, 2015, Mark and I got married. We were making a new life as a blended family.

On that day in November, I stopped at the drug store on my way home from work. When I got back to my car, I noticed a leaf in the shape of a heart by the wheel of my front tire. I felt like it was a sign from Steve that he was with me, that he was sending his love, and that he was happy with the life I was making. I got into my car and smiled. I believed it was Steve communicating with me.

The little things really are the big things.

chapter eleven

About a week after surgery, I get ready to spring from my little nest to go to the follow-up appointment with my medical plastic surgeon, Dr. Ponce. It's nice to get out of the house, even if I am going to a doctor's office.

Mark and I wait in the exam room. While he plays a game on his phone, I sit on the exam table, reflecting pensively, hoping she'll remove some, if not all, of these annoying tentacles protruding from my chest and my sides.

Minutes later, there's a knock on the door. Dr. Ponce steps into the room and gives me a big smile. Her energy and bubbly personality are a lovely break to my wandering thoughts.

"Hello, Emily! How are you doing?" Dr. Ponce beams.

"Hi! I'm feeling good," I say.

"How about we take off those bandages and the wound vac?" She gets right to the point. I appreciate that about her.

I respond with enthusiastic approval. My excitement to get rid of the bandages and the heavy wound vac device are tempered by pangs of anxiety. *How will my breasts look?* I'm not worried about the incisions underneath each breast. I know those will heal. *Do the implants look natural? What about the nipples? Will there be bruises?*

As Dr. Ponce begins to remove the tape holding the bright purple bandages in place, she tells us more about the surgery. She says it not only went smoothly but that I had the most optimal outcome for a mastectomy surgery. The positive news extends beyond being able to have the implants placed right away. Dr. Cunningham removed all of the tissue from both breasts and took a sample of tissue from the right areola. She was able to keep it intact.

"The result then is called a skin sparing and nipple sparing double mastectomy. No other surgery will be needed… that is until the implants have run their course and need to be replaced. That won't be for ten to fifteen years," she says.

Skin sparing and nipple sparing mastectomy. Wow.

The news fills me with relief and gratitude. I'm keenly aware that not every woman has the same outcome from a mastectomy surgery. Some women have to endure a staged reconstruction with tissue expanders to stretch the skin to make room for implants. The expanders require frequent visits to the surgeon to have them filled with saline fluid to help stretch the skin. Other women may have implants placed immediately but aren't able to keep their nipples.

After both bandages are off, Dr. Ponce steps back. "They look wonderful!" She sounds giddy. "What do you think?"

I look down and smile. "Wow! I wasn't sure what to expect, but they don't look much different than before."

I wipe a small tear that's about to escape from the corner of my eye and smile. I feel an incredible sense of relief. I also feel victorious. Not only am I beating cancer but the lasting imprint it will leave on my body will be minimal. I'll have scars, but I'm okay with that. Scars tell a story. They are a mark showing that you've been through something painful, something difficult. But the scar is a sign that you've healed.

A scar is the tattoo of triumph to be proud of.

I'm healing and I'm overcoming this.

On the drive home from the visit with Dr. Ponce, I look at my phone and see I missed a call. I don't recognize the number but whoever it was left a message. I click the message icon to listen to the voicemail. It's from Dr. Cunningham. I press the speaker button so Mark and I can listen to it together.

"Hi, Emily. It's Dr. Cunningham. I don't usually leave messages but it's good news, so I'm happy to leave it. Everything was negative in all of the tissue that we removed during your surgery. It shows the chemo worked. That's fantastic! I look forward to seeing you at your follow-up appointment on Monday."

I let out a little scream of absolute elation and look over at Mark. I really am cancer-free.

"You did it, babe!" Mark's face glows.

Although I knew going into the surgery that the MRI showed there was no evidence of disease, this still feels big. Imaging showed there was no cancer. Now, lab tests show there is no cancer. This feels like the official news that I'm cancer-free.

May 13, 2021. The day I beat breast cancer.

I listen to the voicemail message from Dr. Cunningham a couple of times. I feel like I didn't just beat cancer. I conquered it. I feel strong. It's an amazing feeling. Although I still have more treatment ahead of me, the worst of it is over.

Six months. I began treatment and was deemed cancer-free in six months.

With the bandages off and the drains out, I'm eager to get outside to walk. I feel like it's been ages since I exercised. I just didn't have the energy for much activity at all during chemo, and there were restrictions on how much activity I could engage in after surgery.

As I lace up my shoes, Emma asks where I'm going. "I'm going to take a walk. Do you want to come with me? The weather is so nice." She runs upstairs to get her shoes on. When she comes back down, Stella and our dog, Max, are right behind her.

While Emma gets the leash on Max, I walk through our garage to the driveway. I pause to take a deep breath of the fresh air. I tilt my head upward and feel the sun on my face. It feels glorious—the warmth envelopes me. I hear Max's paws on the garage floor. Emma and Stella follow behind him.

We walk down the driveway to the sidewalk. My legs and joints feel stiff. I'm usually a fast walker, but I won't be speed walking for a bit. I look back and tell the girls to go ahead of me.

"No, Mom. We want to walk with you," Stella says.

"Okay, I'd like that. I'm just moving slower than I thought I would."

Stella gives me a *Seriously, Mom?* kind of look. "You just had surgery ten days ago," she says. I chuckle to myself. I'm so impatient with myself when it comes to recovery. I want to get back to the way I used to be, ready to take a walk or go on a bike ride without a bit of hesitation.

As we get to the corner, past four houses on our street, I stop. Fatigue has washed over my body. "Girls, you two go ahead with Max. I need to go back to the house. I'm really tired."

It's frustrating. I'm not used to my body holding me back from doing what I want to do. Still, I need to listen to my body. It needs rest. By the time I get home, I feel like I walked five miles instead of less than a quarter of one.

Give yourself a break. You need to heal.

There were mornings when I could hardly bear the thought of getting myself out of bed, getting the kids up and moving and out the door before 7:30am to get to school on time. Mornings were tough. There were days when the alarm went off and I wanted to cry. I didn't want to get out of bed. I wanted nothing more than to lay in bed with the covers over my eyes, keeping the sun out. I could sleep. I could hide from the world. If I slept, I didn't have to think about how deeply I missed Steve. Signs of his absence were everywhere. His side of the bed wasn't touched. The covers were still pulled up. There was an empty chair at our dinner table. The chair to his desk was empty. Papers on the desk looked like he would return. His clothes hung in the closet. His tools were organized in our garage.

I couldn't hide for long. I knew three amazing kids were depending on me. How could I lay there with covers over my head when they needed me? I had to keep things as normal as possible. I had to get them off to school. I had to go to work. I was afraid that if I didn't keep us moving in some semblance of a forward direction that they easily could wander down a bad path. I had to keep us going. To get us back to normal as quickly and smoothly as possible.

So, I threw off the covers and got out of bed. I got in the shower. Those moments alone in the shower often brought the tears. I'm not sure why I cried in the shower. Maybe it was being alone. Maybe it was knowing that my cries would be quieted by the sound of the water. Maybe it was the warmth of the water. I always felt a little better with a good cry in the morning. I gave myself a little pep talk. "You can do this. These kids are depending on you."

After I dried off and put on my robe, I walked into Stevie's room to wake him. He always wanted a hug. After a few moments with Stevie, I walked into the girls' room. They often slept together in one of the twin beds. It was so sweet. I woke them with hugs and encouragement.

The mornings were hectic. Some days were easier than others. But mostly, I felt broken. I was trying to navigate my "new normal" as a young widow and solo parent, but I felt so lost. The world around me was the same, yet I felt so out of place. I didn't know anyone my own age, or even close to my age, who was widowed. I was a widow at thirty-five with three young children. No one really understood what I was going through. People could sympathize, but they weren't walking in my shoes. Or even walking a similar path.

Scrolling through Facebook, I came across a graphic about a form of Japanese art called kintsugi. The image and the words in the graphic resonated with me immediately. It was a drawing of a green bowl with gold-colored cracks. Below the bowl were the words, "In Japan, broken objects are often repaired with gold. The flaw is seen as a unique piece of the object's history, which adds to its beauty. Consider this when you feel broken."

As I kept looking at the graphic, something inside of me shifted. While I felt broken and like I was on a piece of ice, drifting away from life that carried on in the distance, the idea of kintsugi gave me a glimmer of hope.

It reminded me that even though it felt like no one really understood what I was going through, people all around me were navigating different challenges—divorce, illness, injury, death of a parent, family member or friend, job loss, and countless other trials that are realities of life. On the outside, it may look like someone has the perfect life, but that person is undoubtedly facing some difficulty—something that makes them feel flawed or broken.

Finding our way through difficult times is a part of life, part of being human. I hated that Steve was gone. I hated that my young children were going to grow up without their dad. How was I going to move forward without Steve? He was the love of my life. He was my husband. He was my partner.

The cracks felt deep. But there was something about kintsugi that made me see strength and beauty in filling the cracks. Nothing could ever or will ever replace Steve. Life was going to go on. I had to move forward. I had to be the one to lead my children forward.

The symbolism of kintsugi is a beautiful reminder that everyone can feel broken by tragedies and difficult experiences, but those difficulties are the cracks that become part of who we are. We carry all of life's experiences, good and bad, with us. They shape us. They become part of our story.

golden scars

Kintsugi is a reflection of how we can endure challenges, setbacks, and hardships, and emerge stronger and more beautiful for having faced them. The use of gold to mend the cracks highlights the idea that our scars, both physical and emotional, can be transformed into something precious and valuable.

I spend the next couple of weeks resting and getting my strength back. Each time I take a walk, I push myself to go a little farther than the day before.

Four weeks off work flies by. I'm ready to get back to work, back to a routine.

The owner of the small marketing agency where I work wants to meet me for coffee before I return to work. I've always had a good relationship with Mallory. Before she joined the agency as president and successor to the founding owner, she was one of my clients.

Mallory has been incredibly supportive of me through my diagnosis and treatment so far. Before I started chemo, we discussed my workload. She put me in the driver's seat, letting me choose the clients and work I felt I could continue to do to support the agency from a PR and marketing standpoint. She also gave me unlimited sick time to use during chemo. Because of that generosity, I never felt guilty taking some time off during an afternoon to rest or not working much the day the bone pain started. I knew I could lean on the rest of the team for support, too. All the support made it easy to keep working while I was going through the first phase of treatment.

As I return to work, she says she wants to help me ease back in. I appreciate the guidance. I've had the tendency to take on too much, especially during stressful times.

We decide to meet at a coffee shop in downtown Sylvania. The downtown area is a lovely quintessential smalltown main street with shops, restaurants, a bakery, a florist, and a coffee shop. As I step out of my car, I feel the warm morning sun mixed with a gentle breeze. It's that perfect start to an early summer day in the Midwest, low seventies. I look over to the coffee shop and see Mallory sitting at one of the tables outside. I realize it's been a long time since I've seen her in person. With the pandemic and working remotely, I've only seen her on a screen through Zoom for the past few months.

As I approach the table, Mallory stands to give me a hug. We walk into the shop to order iced coffees before going back to the table outside to chat. I fill her in on the surgery, recovery, and the last phase of treatment, which will continue for another five months. "I'm excited about coming back to work," I tell her as I take a sip of my drink.

"We are looking forward to having you back," she says. "That's part of the reason I wanted to meet with you before your first day back. I want to make sure we work with you on your workload, so that you don't take on too much."

I thank her and tell her I appreciate her guidance with workload. I remind her that the client work I had been doing prior to my surgery was completely manageable, and I could take on a bit more.

"I'd like you to put together a *30-60-90-day plan*," Mallory says. I'm struck by that term: 30-60-90-day plan. It not only seems formal but unnecessary, in my opinion. It has that feeling of a structure associated with corrective action. I have not had any issues with my work or client relationships.

Likely sensing some apprehension, Mallory tries to allay any concern. "The plan is only intended to guide your return to work. Perhaps you start by resuming client work. Then after several weeks, you might want to resume your work on our content team, writing blog posts. You are our priority. We all want you to succeed."

I thank her for her suggestion and tell her I would create a draft of the three-step plan that she and my supervisor can review.

After some other small talk, we finish our coffee. She mentions needing to get back to her home office to prepare for a call.

Walking back to my car, I'm stuck on this plan. Something about it feels off.

chapter twelve

In the complex and intricate realm of human biology, the battle between life and disease unfolds with us largely unaware. For me, HER2+ breast cancer was lurking below the surface. Before I was aware of its existence as a blueberry-sized lump in my right breast, it was flourishing as I went about life. Physicians, medical researchers, and other professionals in our healthcare system know this age-old struggle of life against disease well. Their perseverance is a testament to the resilience of the human spirit and the ceaseless quest for innovative solutions against disease and its threat to life.

HER2+ breast cancer. This subtype of breast cancer is distinguished by an overexpression of a protein called the human epidermal growth factor receptor 2 (HER2). It's found on the surface of some cells, including cancer cells. The HER2 receptor plays a role in how a healthy breast cell grows, divides, and repairs itself. In some cases, HER2 receptors become hyperactive, stimulating the uncontrolled growth of these cells, leading to the development of tumors. These tumors are often more aggressive and prone to recurrence than other forms of breast cancer. A fierce protagonist, HER2+ breast cancer commands attention, demanding innovative solutions in the battle for survival.

As the cancer progresses, it orchestrates a series of complex biological events. The HER2 protein acts as a conductor, guiding the malignant cells to divide and multiply with alarming speed.

Amidst this tumultuous scene, the immune system tries to quell the activity of the HER2+ breast cancer. However, the malignant cells often manage to evade the immune response, maintaining their relentless onslaught.

Chemotherapy is the first line of defense against the aggression of the HER2+ breast cancer. With advances in treatment for HER2+ breast cancer, immunotherapy and anti-cancer drugs have been added to the mix, specifically Herceptin and Perjeta.

Immunotherapy seeks to amplify the body's own defenses, transforming the immune system into a formidable force of protection. For HER2+ breast cancer, Herceptin and Perjeta are its kryptonite.

Herceptin binds to the overexpressed HER2 protein on the surface of cancer cells. This action acts as a clarion call to the immune system, alerting it to the presence of malignant cells. The immune cells, now awakened to the threat, rush in to neutralize the cancerous intruders.

Perjeta, another member of the immunotherapeutic ensemble, complements Herceptin's plan by blocking the HER2 protein's ability to pair with other HER receptors. This dual threat hinders the cancer's growth and division, creating an interruption in its progression.

Tumor cells are eliminated, and the malignant presence recedes, but lurking in the shadows is the possibility of a HER2+ breast cancer recurrence.

The beauty of this coordinated treatment lies in its preventive measures.

By eradicating the cancerous cells and boosting the immune system's defenses, Herceptin and Perjeta reduce the risk of relapse.

These two powerhouse drugs are already in my arsenal. They were included alongside the two chemo drugs, Taxotere and Carboplatin, in the first phase of treatment. Now, they are the stars of the show as I begin the final phase of treatment.

Knowing how effective this treatment can be against HER2+ breast cancer is an incredible relief. Dr. Al helped to allay my fears early on when he said the three-phase treatment plan has a ninety-five percent cure rate. I am fearful of a recurrence. Although I keep telling myself Mom's cancer was different, she had a recurrence just four months after hearing the words "cancer-free."

Four months. The news came the same day we were moving Steven to Cincinnati. He was about to start his first semester at the University of Cincinnati. When her cancer returned, it came back with a vengeance. Her oncologist told her there were small "spots," a.k.a. tumors, on her liver and right lung. BAM. It was a big blow to all of us.

Before she could begin a new course of chemotherapy, another blow: a small bowel obstruction. Likely a complication from the cancer or the hysterectomy. Correcting the bowel obstruction became priority one. It was as if the cancer had moved to the back burner. Her doctor tried a number of interventions: liquid diet then an NG tube—a tube that went in her nose and to her stomach to suction fluid that was backing up. Surgery wasn't an option. Even though treatment for cancer was in second position, the effects of its rage beneath the surface was evident. Fluid accumulated in her lung. The doctors drained the fluid and did what they could to manage the symptoms.

She was discharged from Cleveland Clinic to a long-term acute care hospital near my parents' home. Her oncologist said she needed time to get stronger so she could resume chemo. He ordered physical therapy. It quickly became apparent, she was far too weak for PT.

Instead of getting stronger so she could resume chemo, it was time for hospice.

This felt like a punch to the gut. Her oncologist said she needed to recover and get stronger to resume chemo. He never used the word "terminal." So we left Cleveland with a sense of hope. Hope that she would get stronger. Hope that she would beat cancer again. Hope that was crushed about five days after getting to the long-term rehab hospital. The hospice nurse spent a few minutes assessing Mom. What her oncologist couldn't or wouldn't tell us about her prognosis, the hospice nurse told us with absolute clarity in a matter of minutes. Mom likely had five days to live.

This cancer is different from Mom's. My treatment plan is different. I've got this. I am the storm.

A total of eleven infusions, one every three weeks. That's thirty-three more weeks of treatment. But the side effects aren't supposed to be as bad as they were with the chemo drugs. Dr. Al says my hair will start to grow back. I should keep my sense of taste, and it should continue to get better. I shouldn't have the horrendous GI symptoms. That certainly takes the sting out of eleven more treatments.

Checking in at the infusion center, it's hard not to feel like I'm getting another round of chemo. I look beyond the registration desk and see all of the treatment cubbies. I remind myself I'm here only to get Herceptin and Perjeta. No chemo. While I sit, waiting to be called back, I tell myself this will be the same but different. It will seem very similar, but the days and weeks following the infusion will be different. My nurse, Nancy, calls my name and escorts Mark and I to the cubby. I take my seat in the recliner and look out the floor-to-ceiling window.

Nancy logs into the computer next to the recliner and confirms the plan for today's treatment. "Just the Herceptin and Perjeta today."

"Yes!" I say with excitement.

"You made it through the roughest part of treatment like a champ," she says. "Your treatments from here on out will be much easier. You won't have the awful side effects. Some patients say they aren't aware of any side effects. And, rather than the four-to-five-hour marathons, these infusions will take about two hours at most."

"That is music to my ears," I say with a laugh.

She goes on to say that I won't need the pre-meds to prevent nausea. Instead, they'll start with saline for about twenty minutes, run the Herceptin and Perjeta together, and finish with about fifteen to twenty minutes of saline. And I don't need the Neulasta patch.

"Halle-freakin-lujah!" I couldn't feel more ready to begin. This feels like a piece of cake compared to what I've been through.

Nancy hangs the small IV bag with saline. I extend the footrest on the recliner and grab my blanket and iPad from my tote bag. I push the button on the bottom of the iPad to display all of the apps. Navigating to the Netflix app, I stop and look out the window. The sky is deep blue, like the ocean. There are small cotton ball clouds scattered across the sky. As I look at the beautiful sky, an immense feeling of calm washes over me. It's as if it finally sets in that the worst part of the treatment is behind me. Lost in my thoughts, Nancy returns to the cubby. She has two IV bags cradled in her arm. Scanning the barcodes on my wristband and the IV bags, Nancy calls over another nurse for the double check—right patient, right medicine, right dosage. While Nancy connects the lines on the IV bags to the line on my port, I finally open Amazon Prime and tap Schitt's Creek.

The episodes are short, only about twenty minutes, so it's easy to watch one after another. Near the end of the second episode, the alarm on the IV pole buzzes. The two IV bags are empty. Nancy returns to disconnect the lines for the IV bags and turns on the saline again.

"Wow, that was fast!"

"Easy, isn't it?" Nancy says. "That's how it will be from here on out."

I can totally do this, especially if there aren't any side effects, or if the side effects aren't bad.

I notice a difference between the days immediately following this last treatment and the previous chemo treatments. I don't feel unusually tired. No nasty GI symptoms. My appetite is starting to come back. My sense of taste is definitely getting stronger. When I'm eating a meal or a snack, I pay attention to the taste. I savor the flavors. I fully appreciate the ability to taste foods again.

One of the lingering side effects of chemo affects me in my everyday life and work. Chemo brain. It's a real thing. There are times when I'm talking and I struggle to find the right word. Sometimes I'll make light of it. If I'm talking to Mark, one of the kids, or my doctor and I can't think of a word, I just say, "Chemo brain." I have to laugh at it. Hopefully, this is a short-term effect. Chemo brain is so very reminiscent of "widow brain." The fog takes me back.

I thought I understood grief. A loved one dies. It's incredibly sad and painful. The firsts are the hardest—the first holidays, the first birthday—and special events, like graduations and weddings. Prior to Steve dying, my experience with losing a loved one included grandparents and more distant family members, like my parents' cousins, or aunts and uncles.

Losing a grandparent or other family member is difficult. Losing a spouse is on a whole different level. When Steve died, it felt like the world stopped. Like my feet were stuck in cement while the world went on as if nothing happened. Like I was living behind a clouded veil, barely able to see anyone else.

I was in shock. I was numb. And as the shock began to wear off, I was left with a deep, empty feeling. Part of me was gone, too. I couldn't comprehend how I was going to move forward. I couldn't think beyond that moment. I didn't want to think beyond that moment. If I did, I'd have to come to the realization that any moment beyond was a moment without Steve. How do you comprehend the gravity of that kind of loss? You stop comprehending life altogether.

I forget things, too. To counteract the forgetfulness, I've been making more lists and notes for myself. Yellow sticky notes look like fallen leaves around my computer. In addition to my list of priorities and to-dos for the week, I also have a list for the list. At the start of each workday, I think about the things I need to accomplish that day—emailing a client, reviewing information prior to a call, working on a blog post, or crunching numbers for a call about client budgets. Lists within lists.

Every couple of weeks, Mallory sends me an invite for a video call to check in to see how I'm doing. I fill her in on how work is going as well as treatment and my recovery. During our call, I mention to Mallory that I have been experiencing some issues with chemo brain, but that I am making adjustments to help myself. I mention my additional lists and notes.

"This is not good, Emily," Mallory says in a bit of a stern tone.

"No, it's okay. This is normal. I just wanted to let you know what I am doing to make sure I stay on top of work and the things I need to be doing. It's working great." I respond quickly, sure of myself. I was just keeping her up-to-date, not warning her.

"No, this is serious. It involves your brain. I am putting you on immediate medical leave," she says and begins to look around her desktop, seemingly readying the paperwork right now.

"But it's not like…" I start to say, but she interrupts me.

"I will send a form to you. Your doctor will need to complete it and provide a date when you can return to work," she says, curt and to the point.

I try to tell her this isn't a big deal, but she won't listen. No checking emails, nothing. Knowing I wasn't getting anywhere, I let her know I have an appointment with my doctor in two days.

We end the call and I slam my laptop shut. This is absolutely ridiculous. There isn't anything wrong with me. So, I need to make extra lists. So what? This is overboard and so unnecessary. She wouldn't even hear me out.

I'm so furious, I don't know what to do with myself. I walk out on our back deck. Sitting on a chair and feeling the warmth of the sun helps me to calm down a bit. I sit outside for a while. A question that has come and gone from my mind for the past few months has shifted front and center. It has my full attention. Do I want to continue working there and doing what I do? It doesn't take long for the answer to come to me. The sound of it reverberates in my mind. No.

If I'm honest with myself, I'm not doing what I love. I love to write. I love creating a strategy to communicate a new service or a new product. I love helping leaders become better communicators. I love the exhilaration of seeing an article in a newspaper or magazine or a story on the news and knowing I helped get it there. I've gotten a lot of experience working at this agency, especially when I was working for my mentor, one of the founding owners. This "new" agency is so different. Now that we're a fully remote agency, the whole vibe is different. The incredible support I felt following my diagnosis and during the first two phases of my treatment is not gone, but something has definitely changed.

Since I can't work, I peruse job sites to see what's out there. While this isn't exactly the ideal time to be looking for a new job, things have changed. Cancer has changed me in many ways. Aside from the obvious changes, it's given me a new perspective on life and what I want with my life, including my career. I want more simplicity. I want to do more writing and communication strategy. What I'm doing just isn't working for me anymore. I'm not fulfilled with my work.

I'm looking forward to seeing Dr. Al and hearing what he has to say about the medical leave. I'm still reeling from my conversation with Mallory. There isn't a problem that necessitates a medical leave, so I can't help but think there's something else going on behind the scenes. It feels like a trap had been set for a while, and I just walked right into it.

While we wait in the exam room to see Dr. Al, I look over the medical form Mallory sent to me. I feel the frustration rising in me again. There's something so unfair about all of this. So demeaning. I'm doing everything I can to get better, but I feel like I'm being punished for something insignificant, something that hasn't affected my work or my clients.

When Dr. Al comes into the room, we talk through my lingering side effects—puffy ankles and joint aches. I mention my experiences with chemo brain and what I'm doing to compensate for the forgetfulness.

"It sounds like you're doing what you should do, making whatever accommodations you need to," Dr. Al says.

"Well, the owner of the marketing agency where I work doesn't agree." Dr. Al makes a face, like he's unsure what I'm saying. "She thinks my forgetfulness might be something serious, something wrong with my brain."

"Are you serious? It's so common and it's temporary," his brow furrows with confusion.

I give the form to Dr. Al. "This is so fucking irritating," he says. "Pardon my language, but I see this far too often. Managers would rather do something that's easier for them rather than help their employee through something like this."

I tell him how supportive Mallory, my boss, and the other members of the team have been up to this point. How generous they've been. How accommodating they've been. That this reaction seems so out of character.

He reviews the form and asks me what I think needs to be done regarding a plan to return to work. I tell him the extra notes and lists I'm making are working for me. He writes on the form as we talk.

"I noted that the accommodations you're making to address the minor forgetfulness that comes with recovery from chemotherapy are sufficient and you'll continue to do this while you feel it's necessary. What date do you want me to list for your return to work?"

Well, since it's already Wednesday afternoon, let's say next Monday," I shrug.

I'm incredibly grateful for Dr. Al's support. His strong reaction surprised me. It was unexpected, but it was good, like he was a fierce protector of me.

I put the signed medical leave form in my bag. After checking out from Dr. Al's office, we go upstairs for another infusion.

Through the summer and fall, my life flows in three-week increments. Between infusions, I continue working and looking for other jobs. I slowly regain my strength. My hair is coming in very curly. Since I had curly hair before, having it grow back in like this isn't a surprise. I don't even consider them to be "chemo curls." I do notice my hair feels thicker and is super grey! I look in the mirror and see a lot of salt and pepper. More and more women are letting their hair go grey, but I don't think I can do it!

My final infusion, the last treatment in my nearly year-long plan to beat cancer, is scheduled for November 12, 2021. Steve's birthday.

Every year on his birthday, I think about how old he would be. This year, he'd be fifty-seven. It's hard to imagine him in his mid-fifties. I picture him having grey hairs mixed in with his brown hair. He'd probably have some wrinkles on his face. But, no doubt, he'd be as handsome as ever! He was forty-four when he died. I am now older than Steve. It's so weird to think that since I was nearly ten years his junior.

There's something special about my final treatment for cancer falling on his birthday. To mark the occasion, and as a thank you to all of the wonderful nurses, I bring sugar cookies. Some of the cookies are decorated with white icing and pink icing in the shape of the breast cancer ribbon. Other cookies are in the shape of a scrub shirt in pink icing with writing that says, "Thank You."

During the treatment, so many of the nurses I had care for me during this past year have stopped by to congratulate me and wish me well. I feel excitement throughout my body. I'm happy and excited the treatment is over. Just beneath the excitement, though, is a sense of fear.

I am cancer-free, but I'll no longer have medicines flowing into my body to keep cancer at bay. I begin to worry about the cancer returning, like it did for Mom, with a vengeance.

I try to remember what Dr. Al said just after I was diagnosed. If I follow the three-phase treatment plan, I could achieve a 95% cure rate. My cancer is gone. I try to hang on to the word "cure."

When the IV bags holding the Herceptin, Perjeta, and saline are empty, the nurse comes back to disconnect the lines from my port.

"It's over," I tell myself. I put any fear of cancer returning to the back of my mind. I want to enjoy the moment of completing my treatment plan. I did it!

Once I gather my iPad, magazines, and blanket, Mark and I walk to the door that leads out of the infusion center. Before walking through the doorway, I pause and look to my left, scanning the treatment area. I won't be back here again. I've been here nearly every three weeks for a year.

When I step through the doorway, I see the nurses lining the hallway toward the elevator. It's time for me to ring the bell. At all cancer centers, the final treatment is celebrated by ringing a bell. The cancer center I go to doesn't have a bell, though. It has a giant gong!

The nurses are clapping and cheering for me as I walk past them and approach the gong. One of the nurses hands me the mallet.

"You've been through a lot, sweetie. Go ahead and hit that gong as loud as you can." They're all smiling for me.

I hold the mallet in my hand. I swing back and then hit the center of the gong. It makes a very low, but very loud sound. I take a moment to relish the thrill of finally hitting the gong and celebrating the end of treatment.

The nurses and other staff congratulate me again before turning back to the infusion center to care for their other patients. Mark walks toward me and gives me a big hug.

As we enter the elevator to leave, the excitement of ringing the gong fades and fear begins to creep in. The doors close, and the air seems to change. There's a static in my ears. The fear. It's everywhere. It's as if I can feel the heaviness of the unfamiliar territory that lies before me.

As the elevator doors slide open, I step out, feeling as if I'm venturing into a barren wilderness on my own, out into the unknown of life post-treatment.

chapter thirteen

My next visit with Dr. Al will be in three months. For some reason, I feel like I am now on my own to figure out what's next. *What about the lingering effects from chemo? What about symptoms of menopause? What if the cancer comes back?* There isn't a cloak protecting me anymore. Herceptin and Perjeta aren't there to help my body stand guard against cancer. While Dr. Al has told me the medications have made recurrence of cancer much less likely, I'm still afraid. It feels like I've been on a boat for a while. Like I've gotten used to the motion of the water. Now that the boat has docked and I've stepped back onto land, I feel off kilter.

I try to put cancer returning out of my mind. Instead, I focus on feeling normal again.

Taking walks is one way I can help my body recover. I love to take walks near our house. There's a wide asphalt path that runs parallel to a street near our house. I used to take the dog for a walk along the path and through a neighborhood back to our house. I could walk a mile and a half without batting an eye. Now, I have to take a shorter route. I'm surprised I can only make it about halfway on this shorter route before I feel complete exhaustion and weakness, needing to go back home. I'm not used to feeling so tired and weak after walking a relatively short distance. When I get back to the house, I share my frustration with Mark.

"I get that it's frustrating for you, but you have to remember what your body has been through in the past year. Chemo touched every part of your body. It's going to take time," he says.

"I know. I'm just not used to having my body flake out on me like this," I say.

"Your body isn't flaking out on you. It needs to heal."

I work on giving myself grace and not being so impatient with myself as my body works to recover from the brutal treatment that coursed through my veins to attack the cancer cells. I promise myself to be okay with where I am now and that it will get better. It's going to be baby steps of progress.

The next morning, my eyes are still closed but I'm aware of the sunlight streaming through the horizontal blinds of my bedroom windows. I open my eyes to see soft yellow rays of light painted on the walls. As I lay in bed for a moment, I feel rested. I feel good.

I sit up in bed and push the sheet and comforter to the side. Suddenly, I notice an odd achy feeling from my neck to my shoulders and down my back to my knees. It's not achy like a cold or the flu is coming on. Rather, I feel as if I aged several decades while I slept. My joints hurt.

What's happening? I felt fine before I went to bed. Worry that I might be coming down with something quickly shifts to irritation. Let me guess, another lingering effect from chemo?

Dr. Al mentioned there could be some persisting effects. I slide to the edge of the bed and let my feet touch the ground. I look at my swollen ankles and sigh. Slowly, I put weight on my feet and stand.

Wow! I feel so old. I take a few steps into the bathroom and pause to look at myself in the mirror. As I look closer at the figure staring back at me, I hardly recognize her. I look pale. My hair is growing back, but it's still so short, and grey.

The short curls remind me of how my hair looked when I was young—a brunette helmet of wild curls. The curls are much tighter now, though. I wonder if I'll have more defined curls and ringlets as my hair continues to grow. It's going to take forever until my hair grows longer, finally reaching my shoulders.

I remind myself, "It's growing back. It will take time." Everything is going to take time. Patience hasn't always been my strong suit. If I'm going to feel like I'm a foreigner in my own skin for a while, I better learn how to be more patient with myself.

I have a feeling this will be easier said than done.

While I'm in the bathroom, I step on the scale and see I've gained a few pounds. As I started eating beyond my meager chemo diet of applesauce, sorbet, bagels, eggs, and mac and cheese, I knew I'd gain back some of the weight I'd lost. During the first phase of treatment with the two harsh chemo drugs, I lost more than fifteen pounds. My clothes hung on me.

Prior to having cancer, I never stepped on a scale. I would get hyper-focused on the number. If the number had gone up, I'd swear off sweets and try to commit to healthier eating. Then, I'd use my clothes as a guide to my weight. I tracked the numbers on the scale as I lost weight through chemo, and I'm tracking it again as I'm gaining it back. I hope I can get back to the number that was on the scale at the time I started treatment. I won't be upset if I come in a few pounds under either!

Moving about in the morning, the stiffness and achiness go away. The swelling in my ankles doesn't go down. I first noticed some swelling when I was going through chemo. My doctor prescribed a diuretic to reduce excess fluid. I thought the swelling was gone, but it's back. I switch from wearing tight leggings to wearing wide leg knit pants to hide my fat ankles.

I'm trying to be patient. What's hard is that, for the most part, I feel good physically. I just want to be back to my old self.

To reduce the swelling in my ankles, I try a remedy that was suggested by a friend. It's a yoga pose. It's called viparita karani, or legs-up-the-wall, which is exactly what it sounds like. I sit on the floor, close to a wall outside my bedroom door. I scooch my butt to the wall, lay down, and extend my legs up the wall. It's a pose that's supposed to be good for circulation.

I'm practicing this yoga pose near the base of the stairs. While my legs are stretched up the wall, Emma and Stella come out of their room and stop at the top of the stairs.

"Mom, what in the world are you doing?" Stella asks with a laugh.

"I heard this could help bring down the swelling in my ankles, so I thought I'd give it a try," I look up at them from the floor.

"Okay! Can I try it, too?" Stella sits next to me and stretches her legs up the wall. She looks over at me and giggles. I look up at my ankles and try to will the swelling to go down. We sit there with our legs extended up the wall for several minutes.

The door from the garage to the house opens and Mark walks into the kitchen. He looks over and sees us.

"What in the world are you doing?" he says with a laugh.

"Trying to get the extra fluid in my fat ankles to go down. I heard this can help."

After a few more minutes of my little yoga session, my attention turns to the grumbling in my stomach. Along with my sense of taste, my appetite is returning to normal.

While Mark, the kids, and I are gathered around our dinner table, Emma asks if the yoga pose helped my swollen ankles.

"I'm not sure," I look down at my ankles and it looks like the swelling may have gone down a bit.

"It's gonna take more than one time," Steven says with a laugh.

The kids know me so well!

Mark suggests I sit in the recliner and elevate my legs while we watch TV. With the high ceiling in our family room, it can get chilly. I grab a blanket and sit in the recliner. Steven reminds me I need to have my legs higher than my heart.

"Thanks, nurse Steven," I say with a smile. He brings two pillows from the couch and helps me get comfortable and in the right position in the recliner.

While we're engrossed in an episode of Ted Lasso, I feel warm. It's a different sensation than just feeling like I don't need the blanket anymore. It's like a blazing fire inside me. An intense heat rises up my torso. My cheeks feel hot. I feel sweat on my forehead. I kick my legs to get the blanket off my feet and toss the blanket to the floor.

Out of the corner of my eye, I see Mark's and the kid's heads turn in my direction.

Mark looks over at me. "What's wrong, babe?"

Confused, I say, "I think I just had my first hot flash!"

It's not at all what I expected a hot flash to be like. I assumed it would be something like sitting outside in the heat and suddenly you feel too warm and need to either jump in a pool or get inside where there's air conditioning. I didn't imagine it would feel like an inferno with flames radiating through my body.

"So, I guess those ovaries of mine didn't rev back up," I say with a little laugh that has more than a hint of irritation. Medical menopause?

"And the hits just keep on coming." Another blow from chemo.

I can't ask Mom about menopause and what it was like for her. I really don't remember her complaining about hot flashes or night sweats. She took hormone replacement therapy. I wonder if that will help. I'll ask Dr. Al about that. There's got to be something I can do to help fan the fire. I ask a few other women I'm close to if they dealt with hot flashes. My aunt said no, but a couple of friends said they did. One friend mentions a supplement that helped her.

At the next appointment with Dr. Al, I wait in the exam room. The topic of hot flashes is front and center of my mind. I try to think of any other issues that have been really bothersome. He steps into the exam room and asks how I'm doing.

"I've been having really bad hot flashes," I blurt out immediately. I can't stand the constant heat in my body.

"Okay, when was your last period?" he asks.

I think back and tell him it's been several months since I had a period.

"It's safe to say you are in menopause," Dr. Al shakes his head, assured.

I knew I had jumped into menopause but hearing it from Dr. Al hits differently. It's real now.

"Okay, well, what can I do about these hot flashes? They're terrible. My mom took hormone replacement therapy. Is that still a thing?"

"Yes, it is, but because of your breast cancer, you cannot take hormone replacement therapy," he says.

"No?" I thought that since my breast cancer wasn't hormone receptor positive that I might be able to take hormone replacements. Feeling a bit defeated, I ask about a treatment a co-worker told me about, bio-identical hormone therapy. It's supposed to be a natural treatment that fills the gaps of what my body is missing.

"No, you cannot do that because of your breast cancer," he says with a stern tone. "There is a supplement that's been shown to help a lot of women. It's called black cohosh."

That's the name of the supplement my friend recommended. Dr. Al goes on to say that it's indicated to help a number of menopausal symptoms, like hot flashes, night sweats, and sleep issues.

I agree to give it a try.

About a week passes, and it occurs to me that my body temperature hasn't suddenly ignited, forcing me to shed blankets or layers of clothes, or step onto our deck to get a shot of cool air. The supplement is a godsend.

I often hear women complaining about hot flashes and night sweats as part of menopause. Some have difficulty sleeping. I don't recall hearing women complain about any other symptoms. So, if I tackled the hot flashes, I'm not having any trouble sleeping, and I don't have periods anymore, maybe a drop into the deep end of the menopause pool isn't that bad after all.

Some of the lingering side effects begin to fade away, too. The swelling in my ankles is gone. The fatigue has lessened. My joints still ache, but I wonder if returning to exercise will help.

I'm getting there. It's a slow road, for sure. I feel like I'm making some progress in the right direction.

One night while we're watching TV, I pick up my phone to do a casual scroll through Facebook. As I scan through posts from friends, I see a post about an exercise program for cancer survivors that will be starting in a couple of weeks. I read through the details: held at the local YMCA, funded by the Livestrong Foundation, no cost to participants. Check, check, check!

This sounds great and comes at the perfect time. Along with the joint aches, the numbers on the scale have been going up. And they've surpassed what I weighed before cancer. I know my body is healing, but I can feel the added weight. It's really noticeable around my stomach. Whenever I've gained weight before, it seemed to settle in my butt and thighs. The fluffiness I feel around my mid-section is uncomfortable, especially when I'm sitting on the couch for a while. It feels like these new rolls around my torso press up against my incisions. In addition to the discomfort, I look down and see the added weight.

Recently, I had been feeling like I was getting back to some sense of normal. Now, I'm feeling like a stranger in my body again. My clothes don't fit. I've had to buy clothes not one but two sizes larger.

Dr. Al has been telling me to "eat right and exercise." I've been eating pretty healthy—more vegetables, for sure. Now, I'm going to start exercising. I hope it makes a difference.

With my energy level increasing, I've been wanting to get back into exercising. I've been a little scared to do anything with weights, though. I need to be careful, especially with my right arm. Because Dr. Cunningham removed three lymph nodes I am at a higher risk for developing lymphedema. It causes swelling due to a buildup of lymphatic fluid. It can cause discomfort and limited mobility. Once it starts, it can be managed, but there is no cure for it. I'm afraid of developing lymphedema.

With the exercise program, I'd be working with trainers who understand how cancer treatment affects the body and how to exercise safely to prevent lymphedema. This feels like the perfect way to get back into exercising safely.

I'm excited for my first exercise session. I'm ready to get out of the house and looking forward to working out with other cancer survivors.

As I look through the stacks of leggings, tank tops, and sports bras I haven't worn in so long, I feel a sense of conviction and determination.

I change into a pair of black leggings and a tank top. With my running shoes on, I'm ready!

As I walk into the lobby of the Y, I hear tennis shoes squeaking on the tile floor and inhale that smell of chlorine and humidity from the indoor pool to my left. Kids are running around excitedly. I approach the desk. A young woman working at a computer looks up and greets me. I give her my name and tell her I'm there for the Livestrong exercise program. She gives me directions to get to the fitness center.

I'm guided into a room with about eight other people. I take a seat next to a woman who I guess is a few years older than me. The three trainers walk to the front of the room and introduce themselves. They take turns sharing some information about the program. After we get the lowdown on the baseline assessments, length of each session, and the plan to start with cardio machines and work up to weights, the lead trainer asks each person to introduce themselves.

The group is divided into three smaller groups and assigned to a trainer. Each group is taken into the fitness center. As we walk through the doors of the fitness center, I get an immediate sense of hope.

Since I had exercised with weights before my cancer treatment, my trainer, Rory, said it would be okay for me to begin using weights as long as we start off with light ones. The first step is to warm up. I've never been a big fan of cardio. I've used treadmills and elliptical machines in the past. It's a chore for me to exercise on those machines. I decide to try out a stationary bike. I will the hop on the bike and try to navigate the giant screen in front of me. There are pre-set workouts, virtual trails, and buttons to access Netflix, Facebook, or other apps. I pick a trail that looks like I'm riding on a hilly path by the water. After about ten minutes riding a stationary bike, I felt warmed up enough to venture over to the weights.

Rory meets me by the chest press machine. We talk about how to begin slowly, and he suggests I begin with some arm exercises using free weights. I walk behind him to the row of free weights at the back of the fitness center. The back wall is one giant mirror. As I get closer to the mirror, I see my reflection. I immediately look away.

Is that what I look like? Ugh! I know I've gained some weight, but...

I can't look at myself. Obviously, we have mirrors at home, but not as big as this one. I'm horrified at my reflection. I look way heavier than I thought I did. I knew I had put on some weight. Seeing myself in the full-length mirror crushes me. The sense of hope I had walking into the fitness center just fifteen minutes ago has been crushed.

I walk over to the row of weights and pick up a set of five pound weights. Instead of looking at myself in the mirror, I turn around to begin doing the bicep curls. The rest of the workout, I avoid the giant mirror.

I drive home trying not to focus on the memory of my reflection in the mirror at the gym. As much as I try to put it out of my mind, I can't. I hear Dr. Al's advice: "Eat right and exercise." That's what I'm trying to do, but it's not working. I am glad that I see Dr. Al for my six month follow-up tomorrow. Maybe he'll have more advice for me.

I tell Dr. Al about the lingering side effects—what's gotten better and what's still hanging on. I tell him I want to talk about my weight. He walks over to the computer to look at the numbers the nursing assistant entered into the computer.

"Okay. I see what you weighed today. Let me take a look at the trend of your weight over the past year." He clicks the mouse a few times. "Emily, you've gained thirty pounds in the past year! That's not good."

"I'm well aware of that," my response comes out a little louder than I anticipated. "I have been doing what you said. Eat right and exercise. I'm eating healthier than I ever have and I've been doing a strength training class at the Y. But the numbers on the scale keep going up. What can I do?"

"Keep doing what you're doing, eat right and exercise. It's going to take time. I'm sure menopause is playing a role in this. Just keep at it. I wish there was a magic pill, but there's not."

Dr. Al tries again to give me some words of encouragement. "You can do this. Give yourself time. Remember, your body has been through a lot and it's still healing."

I know my body has been through a lot, but I finished chemo a year ago. I thought my body would have bounced back to normal by now. As we walk to the car, I feel as defeated as ever. I thought Dr. Al would have something more specific to say. If not, at least refer me to the hospital's weight loss program. But nothing.

Angry. I feel angry. I'm surprised by it, but I shouldn't be. Just when I thought cancer was done with me, my entire body continues to be hijacked by this disease, thrown into menopause before its time, and it seems like I'll never feel normal again. I welcome the anger. I know I need to take things into my own hands now.

chapter fourteen

Right after Steve died, *I was more concerned about getting the kids into see a grief counselor than seeing one myself. They were so young.*

After a couple of years, I decided it was time to do some grief counseling myself. I was overwhelmed with the day-to-day solo parenting. I missed Steve so much. I was trying to grow in my career. It was a lot to handle.

The first session with the grief counselor seemed so awkward. I wasn't sure where to start or what to say exactly. I told her about Steve's struggles with mental illness and how he was doing everything he should to get better. Yet, I blamed his doctor. She kept trying different antidepressants over the course of several months. In some instances, it didn't seem like she gave some of the medicines enough of a chance to work. Four different antidepressants in six months seemed like too much.

I felt the frequent change in medications is what contributed to his death. I shared this with the counselor. I told her I was angry with the doctor.

She asked me if I was angry with Steve.

I said no. I felt so much sympathy for what Steve was trying to carry on his own. He put on such a brave face, yet I couldn't imagine how much he was hurting on the inside. I was right there, by his side. I remember telling him one time that we were living our vows, especially the part about in sickness and in health. I promised him that I would be there, doing everything I could to support him. And I did.

When the counselor asked me if I was angry at him, I was taken aback. I didn't want to betray Steve in any way. I was thinking of what he was going through. I know he didn't open up to me about everything. Still, I felt protective of Steve and his memory.

She told me, "I want to push you to get angry at him." Then, she reminded me that I had promised to stay by Steve's side. I was there for him in sickness and in health, but he was the one who left. He left me behind. He left me alone with the kids.

I struggled with this initially. I felt bad at the idea of being angry with him. He was gone. He had struggled with so much mentally. But, as I worked through my feelings and loosened my grip on my protection of him, I did get angry. I felt like he abandoned me.

It wasn't fair. I was in it to the very end. I just never imagined the end would come so soon—just a few months before we'd celebrate our ten-year wedding anniversary.

My anger came and went. When something happened with the kids, good or bad, I found myself looking up to the sky. What I said changed each time.

"Damnit, Steve, why aren't you here to help me with addressing bad grades?"

"Why aren't you here to help me with the kids, especially when the girls decide to cut their hair or spill nail polish on their carpet?"

"Steve, why the hell aren't you here to watch Stevie begin high school or be here for the girls' confirmation or to watch the kids walk across the stage to get their high school diplomas?"

I had to get to the bottom of the well of my anger so I could live with the grief. I had to tell Steve why I was mad, and tell him often. He knew it was because I loved him so much. That rage was born of deep love.

Hearing Dr. Al say that I need to keep doing what I'm doing and to give myself time to heal is frustrating. It's been one year since I had my final chemo treatment. It's been five months since I had my last infusion of Herceptin and Perjeta. My hair is growing longer. Exercising regularly has helped me to increase endurance when I work out and reduce joint pain. Taking the black cohosh supplement has practically eliminated hot flashes and night sweats. Sleeping at night isn't a problem.

Reflecting on this wild journey of breast cancer and taking stock of what I've been through and how far I've come is empowering. I feel incredible strength in what I've been through. I've been working at giving myself grace in the area where I'm still struggling... weight gain.

The two side effects from treatment that impacted me the most, making me feel so exposed, so self-conscious, were losing my hair and gaining so much weight. These were the side effects that I could see. People who know me could see them, too. People I don't know could see them. The hair loss in particular branded me a cancer patient. The weight loss was more of a self-imposed scarlet letter of sorts. I know I was far more focused on my weight than anyone else. During the fall and winter months, it was easy to hide the extra weight with my clothes. Sweaters and longer jackets hid the fluff. Now entering spring, I feel more exposed. Just eating right and exercising is not cutting it.

When Mark and I get back home from seeing Dr. Al, we sit in the family room and talk. The TV is on in the background. As we talk, I overhear a commercial about a weight loss program. I interrupt Mark and ask him to grab the remote and replay the commercial. I scoot forward in my seat. It's from a local weight loss clinic that provides customized plans to help people lose weight. As the announcer talks about the clinic's approach and a woman who had lost forty pounds shares her experience, I feel a twinge of excitement. This is it. This is what I need.

I'm not going to settle for this new version of me. I grab my phone and call the number on the screen. As soon as the woman on the other end of the phone says, "Hello, Medical Weight Loss Clinic, this is Allison, how can I help you?" I feel hope.

I explain my situation—breast cancer, chemo, medical menopause, thirty-pound weight gain. "Is this something you could help me with?" I ask with some trepidation.

"Yes, we absolutely can help you. We've had other clients who've had cancer as well as many women who've experienced weight gain from menopause," she says.

I feel relief and hope. I schedule a consultation to learn more about the program.

While there is only so much I can do with my hair as it grows back, I feel like I'm grabbing hold of the reins of this weight gain.

Within a few minutes of talking with the consultant at the weight loss clinic, I know it is something I can do. She walks me through the plan, which outlines the amounts of protein, fruits, vegetables, dairy, and starches to eat each day, as well as protein bars and a large amount of water. The consultant is so encouraging and tells me that if I follow the plan, I can lose the weight. It's the first time in a long time that I have hope that I can lose the weight. I've got a real plan.

I've taken a firmer grip on the reins of the trajectory of my career, too. During the past few months, I've been disheartened about work. It's not the work itself. I've been incredibly proud of the work I've been doing—leading marketing and communications strategies for clients and assisting with the development of a new marketing campaign for a client. It's definitely not the work, but how I'm feeling about where I work.

Ever since I told Mallory and the rest of the team the pathology report from surgery showed there was no evidence of cancer, there's been a shift with Mallory. Any interactions I have with her seem strained. This came into clear focus when I made the "executive" decision as the account lead to send a statement of work to a client. It was supposed to be a quick overview of the work we'd be doing. Given the scope of the work, it didn't need to be a formal plan. Mallory wanted to get it to the client by noon the following day. I took the lead to coordinate with other team members who would be contributing to the work. As I read the draft of the statement of work, it looked great. I messaged the team to see if anyone had any changes to make before we sent it to our production coordinator for proofing. I waited a bit but heard nothing. Feeling some pressure to get it to the client by noon, and it was already pushing one o'clock, I sent it to the client. After hearing crickets for so long, Mallory messaged me asking why I sent the document to the client.

Shit.

Relaying her need for it to be a quick summary of the work and the pressure to get it to the client by noon didn't seem to matter. She was pissed.

This was it. This was going to be *the thing* that she could point to, and I'd be out. I'd seen it before with other former coworkers. While she says she likes to see account leads take control and getting work done, that wasn't the case here.

Going through major life events like cancer, the death of a spouse, being a solo parent, and helping kids navigate grief has given me a perspective on what's really important in life. I've had an epiphany. This stuff at work isn't important in the grand scheme of things. I'm not happy there. I've been looking for other opportunities for a while. I've been taking stock of where I've been in my career and what I want going forward.

Still, I was surprised when I got an instant message from Mallory. It read, "Time for a quick chat?" Five words that instilled instant panic. "Sure," I responded.

I wait nervously for the notification to join the video call. Once I hear that all too familiar chime, I click the "Join" button. The video begins and I see Mallory sitting at her desk.

I start to say hello, but she cuts me off.

"You're not happy here," she says.

"Wait, what? What are you talking about?" I am stunned by her statement.

"You're not happy here. I've been going through the results of the quarterly employee survey, and I just know you're not happy," she says.

"You're not happy and we've had some difficulties lately, particularly with the document that went to the client before I had a chance to finish my edits. I think it's time that we agree to part ways."

"Uh, no," I say firmly. "I am not agreeing to part ways. You called me telling me that I'm not happy. So, are you letting me go?"

"I think it's for the best," she says.

"Fine."

Mallory ends the call with some details about a severance package and tells me she'll write up something announcing my departure to share with the team. She said she'd send the draft to me to review before the announcement goes to the team.

I click the "Leave" button.

You've got to be fucking kidding me. She fired me. I'm still finishing treatment for cancer, and she let me go.

I'm pissed off. Not that I'm no longer employed. I'm pissed that I didn't find another job first and could tell her I was quitting.

I re-center. It's over and that's what matters. I've been wanting a new job, something that allows me to do more communications strategy and writing. I'm happiest when I'm doing that kind of work—work that challenges me, builds my confidence. Rather quickly, my attitude changes from anger to an incredibly wonderful feeling of being free. I'm free, but there's also an oh crap feeling. I have two months of severance. Two months to find what's next for me professionally.

While I've been looking for a new job, I've also considered starting my own PR consulting company.

Conversations with my mentors and other colleagues helped to solidify the direction for my consultancy. They even introduced me to people who were in need of communications and writing support. Two and a half months after the "you're not happy" conversation with Mallory, and three days before Christmas, I file paperwork to establish Clarion Communications, LLC.

In so many ways, I had closed a hundred chapters of my life. I had been through so much—the death of my husband, of my mom, through parenting alone, through cancer, and through a cascade of losses that seemed to pile on top of me at every turn. So, taking control of my own career, of my own dreams, felt like the most control I'd had in a very long time. And I was proud. Deeply proud of myself. I knew Steve and Mom were proud of me, too.

I've come out on the other side of all these things a changed and better woman. And I've said goodbye to everything and everyone I've lost while holding the deepest gratitude for how they've each shaped me into who I am. Whenever Steve and I talked about our end-of-life plans—plans I imagined were for when we were both very old together—he always jokingly mentioned that he didn't want to be buried. Something about taking up space on this earth when he was alive, and that he didn't want to take up more space after he died. That his ashes could be scattered in the lake, become food for fish. But I need Steve to know that he's never stopped taking up space on this earth and in my life. That he'll always be with us through everything.

Needless to say, when Steve died, I knew what he wanted. I wasn't sure how I felt about it. Other family members who had died were buried in cemeteries. We'd go to the cemetery to feel like we were with a part of them. If Steve was going to be cremated, would I still feel that kind of connection to him?

As I was planning the funeral, the funeral director suggested that I bury a portion of the ashes and then scatter the rest. I loved the idea. I felt like I could have a place to go to be with a part of him. I wasn't sure if looking out on the lake would give me the same feeling of connection.

My dad connected with a friend of his who had a sailboat. He said it would be an honor for him to take our family out on his sailboat so that we could scatter Steve's ashes.

We had two ceremonies to bury Steve—one at a cemetery near my house and the other on a beautiful sailboat on Lake Erie. It was a perfect summer day. My family and Steve's family gathered with Father Dave at a marina in Sandusky. We boarded the sailboat and had a lovely sail on the lake. The captain of the boat asked if there was a place we had in mind where we wanted to scatter Steve's ashes. He suggested we sail toward the Marblehead Lighthouse. That was perfect. I've always loved lighthouses. The symbolism is perfect. My guiding light.

As we sailed toward the lighthouse, I held a heart-shaped box that contained the majority of Steve's ashes. The box seemed to be made of papier-mâché. The funeral director told me that after I placed the box on the surface of the water, it would float for a bit. As it took on more water, the box would sink and eventually disintegrate, allowing the ashes to scatter beneath the surface.

The captain dropped the anchor just off the coast of the lighthouse. Father Dave said a few prayers and blessed the ashes. I placed the box on the surface of the water. Then, the kids and I tossed white roses in the water. The box bobbed on the surface of the water for a bit. After a few minutes, the box absorbed more and more water. Then, it sunk below the surface.

As I watched the box drop into the water, I felt a rush of sadness. It felt like I literally let Steve fall from my hands and slip away out of sight. The last physical part I had of him was gone. Through tear-filled eyes, I looked at the lighthouse. It was then that I felt a deep connection to the lighthouse. It was near the place where I set Steve's ashes to be free. As my eyes reached the top of the lighthouse, I prayed that Steve was at peace. I desperately wanted him to be with me. But if I couldn't have that, I just wanted to know he was at peace, no longer suffering.

As I looked at the lighthouse, I tried to imprint every feeling, every sense on my heart. I felt the warmth of the sun on my shoulders. I felt the breeze move across my face and move through my hair. I felt Steve's presence there. It was hard to peel my gaze away from the lighthouse. I could have stayed there forever.

After some time, the captain announced he'd be pulling up the anchor and we'd be sailing back to the marina. As the sailboat moved across the water away from the lighthouse, I found myself looking back toward the lighthouse many times. It felt like I was leaving part of Steve behind. I thought about him being free, being part of the lake he loved so much. Through tears, I smiled.

The kids and I return to the lighthouse often. We visit on the anniversary of his death. Other times, I suggest to the kids that we go to the lighthouse. There were times they didn't want to go. Maybe they'd rather play with friends. One Friday evening, I asked the kids if they'd like to get pizza and visit the lighthouse. At first, they said no. Then, the kids asked if they could bring some friends from our neighborhood. Stevie, Stella, Emma, and I, along with two other kids, loaded up in my car and headed to the lake. We stopped for pizza. It was so fun to listen to the kids talk about silly things and giggle. After we finished eating, we drove out to Marblehead and to the lighthouse. The kids ran toward the large rocks that line the coast. They had a ball jumping from rock to rock. While they were having fun, I took some time to just be… looking up at the lighthouse and gazing at the water. I felt a sense of comfort being there. I felt Steve all around us.

Coming to the other side of the major storm that was cancer, I feel a new connection to the lighthouse. It's a symbol of the constant presence, support, protection, and watchful eye of Steve and Mom.

"Fate whispers to the warrior "You cannot withstand the storm" and the warrior whispers back "I am the storm".

\- Unknown

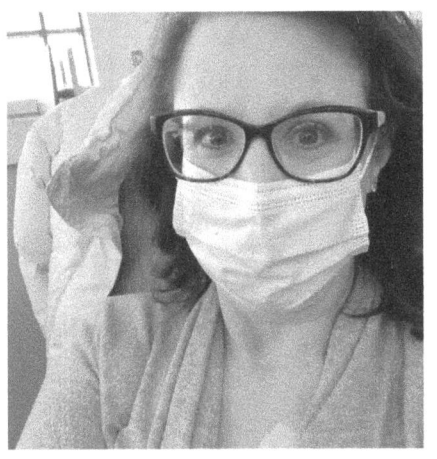
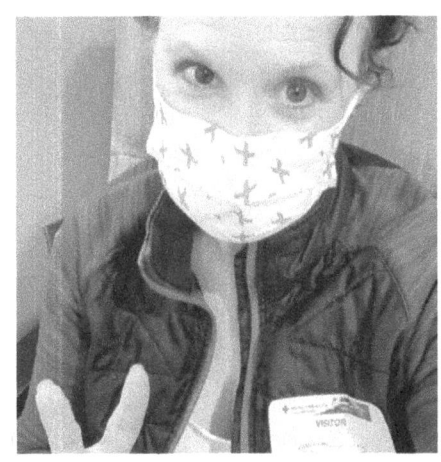

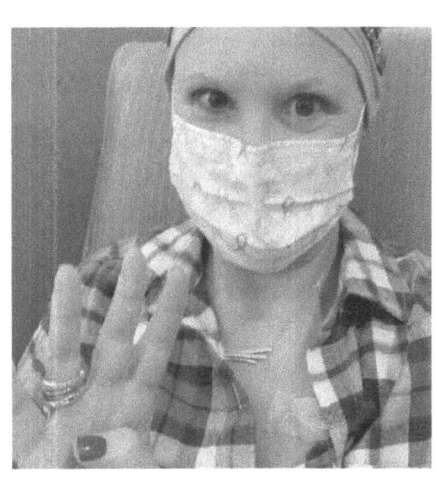

"She nurses her scars into a force full of stars, aware that only she can turn them into light."

- Angie Weiland-Crosby

"Do not grieve. Anything you lose comes around in another form."

\- Rumi

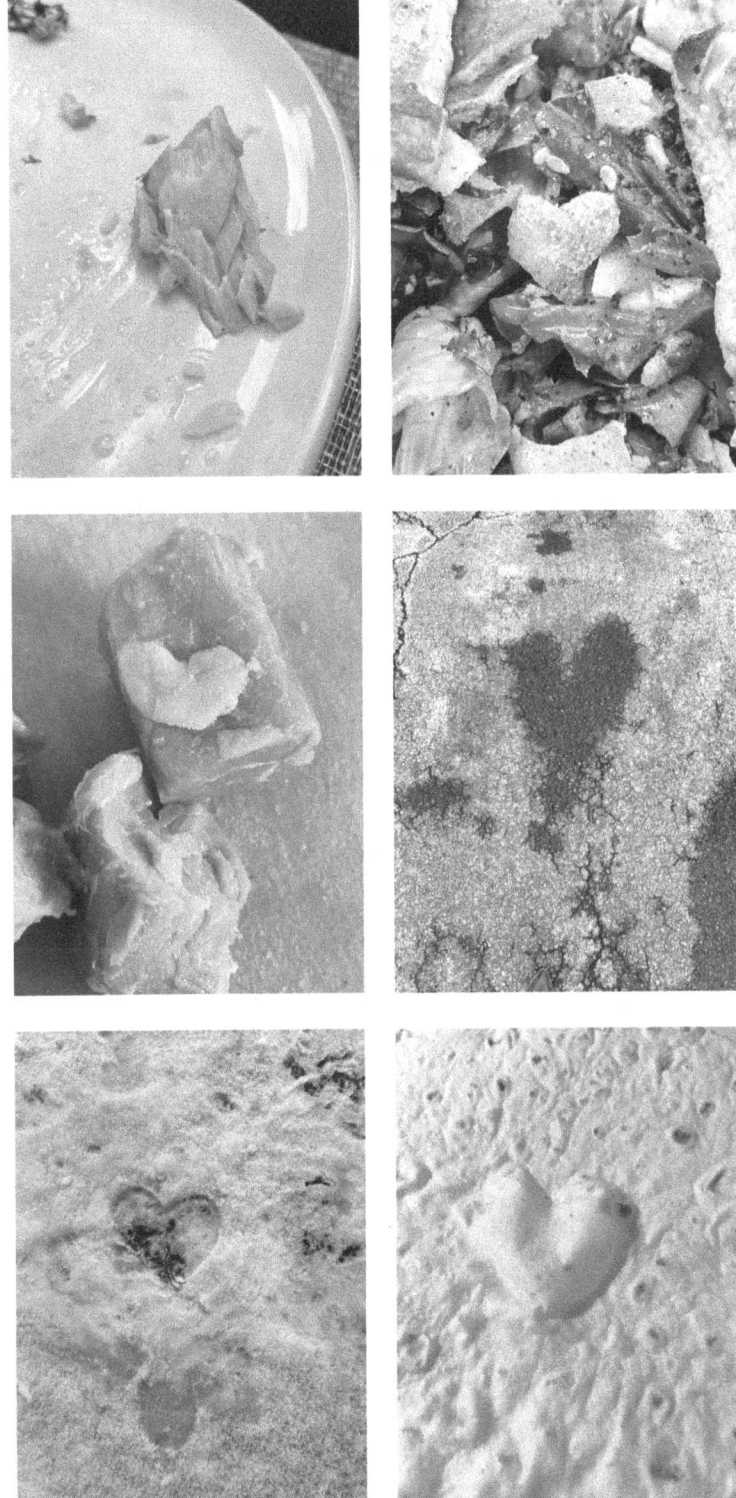

"I am the storm."

Emily (Barry) Zarecki is a seasoned public relations and communications professional. Her 25-year career spans global Fortune 500 and Fortune 1000 companies, nonprofit and agency settings.

Following treatment for breast cancer, Emily sought to make a career change. In late 2021, she founded Clarion Communications, a strategic communication and public relations consultancy.

Passionate about a few causes close to her heart – mental health, suicide prevention and breast cancer awareness – Emily has served on the board for Unison Health in Toledo, OH and supported fundraising efforts for NAMI Toledo in memory of her husband. As a recent breast cancer survivor, Emily is enthusiastic about advocating for research and education about breast cancer and eliminating disparities in access to diagnostics and treatment. She serves as an advocacy ambassador for Susan G. Komen.

Emily also serves as President for the PRSA Northwest Ohio Chapter and is a member of Rotary Club of Toledo, the Press Club of Toledo and Women of Toledo/HerHub. She is also a founding member of Chicks for Charity and Toledo Women for Good.

She resides in Sylvania, Ohio with her family.